"I have always loved wh[...] ing this book by my frie[...] book is theologically ric[...] I had not previously con[...] reading of this book to [...]

Daniel L. Akin, president, Southeastern Baptist Theological Seminary

"Andy Davis has created a wonderful resource reflecting on what our lives will be like in heaven. He pulls insights from Bible passages that give us a glimpse into the kinds of activities God will continue throughout our time in eternity, and he makes a clear case that much of Scripture has implications for life in heaven. The picture he paints will leave you longing even more for our eternal home."

Kevin Ezell, president, North American Mission Board, Southern Baptist Convention

"Andy Davis encourages us with the hope of heaven that is promised, showing from Scripture and with many helpful illustrations and stories that our future will be dazzling and thrilling. What makes Davis's work especially compelling is that he explains how the hope of heaven transforms our lives now. Read and be encouraged and challenged."

Thomas Schreiner, associate dean of the School of Theology and James Buchanan Harrison Professor of New Testament Interpretation and Biblical Theology, The Southern Baptist Theological Seminary, Louisville, Kentucky

"As with any good book on the subject, this one will make you homesick for heaven. But beyond that, it will increase your resolve to pursue and enjoy God and the things of God even more fervently now. I was astonished at the number of fresh insights Andy Davis provides in this Scripture-saturated book. The pages are packed with stories—both well-known and little-known—from Christian history that deeply affected me. The message of this book is illustrated in such fresh ways, especially by some of the author's personal experiences. Doctrine and practice are masterfully woven together from beginning to end. I've never been so encouraged, convicted, enlightened, made hopeful, and delightfully surprised by a book on heaven like this one."

Donald S. Whitney, professor of biblical spirituality and associate dean, The Southern Baptist Theological Seminary, Louisville, Kentucky, and author of *Spiritual Disciplines for the Christian Life*, *Praying the Bible*, and *Family Worship*

"I'm so grateful to Andy Davis for his rich, pastoral meditations on heaven. In *The Glory Now Revealed*, Andy shows from Scripture and the best of the Christian tradition that our glorification will include a much fuller understanding of how God was always at work during our particular earthly journeys and throughout all of redemptive history. Reading this book only causes me to long more for that day when I experience that beatific vision and when all of my sins, shortcomings, sufferings, sorrows, and sicknesses are no longer my present reality but rather are fully redeemed parts of my testimony—to the praise of God's glorious grace!"

Nathan A. Finn, provost and dean of the university faculty,
North Greenville University

"In this powerfully enlightening and hope-filled book, Andy Davis asks the question, How much heaven do you want? You may think that strange, until you've read his portrayal of what awaits the child of God in the age to come. This is the best and most biblical book on heaven I've read, and it prompted me to shout aloud, in answer to his question, 'All of it!'"

Sam Storms, PhD, lead pastor for preaching and vision,
Bridgeway Church, Oklahoma City, Oklahoma

"In *The Glory Now Revealed*, Andy Davis seeks to unroot us from this world and cause us to long for heaven by reminding us that our eternity is not a static existence but an eternal learning of God and his mighty works throughout history in and for his people that will magnify his glory. If you want to be of any earthly good in this world, read this book. It will cause you to long for heaven and pray for the coming of God's eternal kingdom in Christ."

Juan R. Sanchez, senior pastor, High Pointe Baptist Church,
Austin, Texas, and author of *The Leadership Formula: Develop the
Next Generation of Leaders in the Church*

"Even as we desire to be more heavenly minded, we struggle with exactly on what we should think and ponder. Thankfully, Andrew M. Davis's new book, *The Glory Now Revealed*, arrives as a trusted guide to help. This book does more than just direct your gaze to what is right and true in heaven, it stirs your heart and affections for the God who is both there and near."

Jason G. Duesing, provost and professor of historical theology,
Midwestern Seminary, Kansas City, Missouri

"This book stirred up every bone in my body. This is not another fanciful and speculative treatise on heaven. This is a book about the endless delight that awaits those who know Jesus. From the first sentence to the last, it raised my affections for God, filled me with gospel hope, compelled me into mission, and deeply increased my longing for heaven. I am going to ask every member of my church to read this book!"

J. Josh Smith, pastor, Prince Avenue Baptist Church, Athens, Georgia

THE GLORY NOW REVEALED

WHAT WE'LL DISCOVER ABOUT GOD IN HEAVEN

ANDREW M. DAVIS

BakerBooks

a division of Baker Publishing Group
Grand Rapids, Michigan

© 2021 by Andrew M. Davis

Published by Baker Books
a division of Baker Publishing Group
PO Box 6287, Grand Rapids, MI 49516-6287
www.bakerbooks.com

Printed in the United States of America

All rights reserved. No part of this publication may be reproduced, stored in a retrieval system, or transmitted in any form or by any means—for example, electronic, photocopy, recording—without the prior written permission of the publisher. The only exception is brief quotations in printed reviews.

Library of Congress Cataloging-in-Publication Data
Names: Davis, Andrew M. (Andrew Martin), 1962– author.
Title: The glory now revealed: what we'll discover about God in heaven / Andrew M. Davis.
Description: Grand Rapids, MI: Baker Books, a division of Baker Publishing Group, 2021. | Includes bibliographical references.
Identifiers: LCCN 2021009231 | ISBN 9781540901040 (paperback) | ISBN 9781540901941 (casebound) | ISBN 9781493430277 (ebook)
Subjects: LCSH: Glory of God—Christianity. | Heaven—Christianity.
Classification: LCC BT180.G6 D38 2021 | DDC 231—dc23
LC record available at https://lccn.loc.gov/2021009231

Unless otherwise indicated, Scripture quotations are from The Holy Bible, English Standard Version® (ESV®), copyright © 2001 by Crossway, a publishing ministry of Good News Publishers. Used by permission. All rights reserved. ESV Text Edition: 2016

Scripture quotations labeled CSB are from the Christian Standard Bible®, copyright © 2017 by Holman Bible Publishers. Used by permission. Christian Standard Bible® and CSB® are federally registered trademarks of Holman Bible Publishers.

Scripture quotations labeled HCSB are from the Holman Christian Standard Bible®, copyright © 1999, 2000, 2002, 2003, 2009 by Holman Bible Publishers. Used by permission. Holman Christian Standard Bible®, Holman CSB®, and HCSB® are federally registered trademarks of Holman Bible Publishers.

Scripture quotations labeled KJV are from the King James Version of the Bible.

Scripture quotations labeled NASB are from the (NASB®) New American Standard Bible®, Copyright © 1960, 1971, 1977, 1995, 2020 by The Lockman Foundation. Used by permission. All rights reserved. www.lockman.org

Scripture quotations labeled NIV are from THE HOLY BIBLE, NEW INTERNATIONAL VERSION®, NIV® Copyright © 1973, 1978, 1984, 2011 by Biblica, Inc.® Used by permission. All rights reserved worldwide.

All italics in direct Scripture quotations are the author's emphasis.

The author is represented by the literary agency of Wolgemuth & Associates.

Baker Publishing Group publications use paper produced from sustainable forestry practices and post-consumer waste whenever possible.

21 22 23 24 25 26 27   7 6 5 4 3 2 1

To my five children—
Nathaniel, Jenny, Carolyn, Calvin, and Daphne.
Your mom and I have no greater joy
than knowing you are all walking in the Truth.

Contents

Introduction

The book you are about to read is intended to be a foretaste of heaven. I yearn for it to be a journey of hope for you, because this world we are living in is drowning in a sea of hopelessness. People who do not know the grace of God through faith in Christ are said to be "without hope and without God in the world" (Eph. 2:12 CSB). It is a devastating thing to be hopeless, because human beings are wired to be essentially forward-looking in our outlook. If we are truly convinced that the future is bleak, it is difficult to take another step in life. The Bible reveals that God has woven a sense of eternity into the hearts of all people (Eccles. 3:11), and that means we are constantly thinking about the future—where we are heading—and (perhaps secretly) even more about our eternal future.

Where We Begin

There are many conceptions about heaven floating around the worldwide marketplace of ideas. But only a biblical vision of heaven, constructed carefully from passages of God's perfect Word, will in the end prove to be true. To conceive of a heaven based on vain imaginings and false doctrine will only lead many further on a path to destruction. But to drink in a pure vision of heaven based on Scripture will build within us a hope that does not disappoint (Rom. 5:5).

In this book, we will learn about a heaven that is dynamic and eternally fascinating, and in which a large part of our experience will be continually learning more aspects of the glory of God. For most of my Christian life, I have had a defective view of heaven as being essentially static, in which we have been made perfect at death and learn in that instant everything we need to know about God, and then spend eternity basically in one place singing praise songs to God. As I have talked to other Christians, I have come to realize that this is how most of them viewed heaven as well.

No one wants to admit that this sounds boring and that such thoughts are actually a little depressing. Several people told me they just try to keep it simple: "I figure we'll just die, go to heaven, and be happy. End of story."

But I have found that this "boring" view of heaven is defective and unbiblical. And because it is defective and unbiblical, it is not very helpful for feeding Christian hope. Most of us have received a view of our eternal home that is truly disappointing. But "hope does not disappoint." So it is time for us Christians to roll up our sleeves, work on the texts, and discover a dynamic view of heaven that will electrify us, empowering us to grow in holiness and be energetic in sharing this hope with desperately lost people all around the world.

Jesus said to the Sadducees (who had a defective view of the afterlife as well), "You are wrong, because you know neither the Scriptures nor the power of God" (Matt. 22:29). Journey with me to find out how much more the Scriptures have said about our eternal heavenly home than we have known before.

It is my deepest desire that this journey will energize your heart as never before to yearn for heaven, to store up treasure in heaven, and to rescue as many people as possible to join you in heaven.

Where We Are Headed

Now it is time to begin our discovery of some of what the Bible reveals about our future eternal home. We will walk through it step-by-step, looking at various aspects in turn. We will begin by seeking to prove from sound scriptural exegesis that we will remember earth's events in heaven (chapter 2). Then we will describe the astonishing transformation of our bodies, minds, and hearts in glorification, and how that transformation will make our eternal education in God's glory so perfectly satisfying to us (chapter 3).

In chapter 4, I will seek to argue that God will not merely tell us what he did in the past but will actually have the power to show it to us by vision. In chapter 5, we will discuss the powerful concept of heavenly rewards, and how these rewards will be directly tied to how we lived our lives on earth and will essentially afford unequal experiences of God's glory in heaven. In chapter 6, we will trace out with maddening brevity the stunning complexity of all of human history, knowing that in heaven alone will we have the time and capacity to take in the scope and dimensions of all the centuries and all the nations of history. Chapter 7 unfolds how all the heroes of church history will be properly honored in heaven. By contrast, chapter 8 focuses on obscure people and movements of church history, and how God will reveal what he did in and through each one. Chapter 9 discusses how God will finally reveal the spiritual dimensions—the angels and demons—of every single day of redemptive history. In chapter 10, we will have a foretaste of the heavenly review of our own personal lives—how God worked in us personally for his purposes.

Chapters 11 through 13 cover the three hardest topics for this concept of heavenly review: our sins, our sufferings, and the damned. Chapter 14 will make the case that remembering the history of evil in this world will be eternally essential to our hating it forever. Finally, chapter 15 concludes with an exhortation to gain as much of heavenly glory as we can by faith-filled exertions now.

Ready? Let's begin this journey together!

CHAPTER 1

Lost Treasures Reclaimed

For the countless multitude of the redeemed, heaven will be an eternal education in the glories of God. The redeemed will drink from an endless river of his glory, eat from a delightful tree of his glory, tour a vast museum of his glory, view a visionary theater of his glory, explore a limitless universe of his glory, bow before the throne of his glory, and stare unblinking and unblinded into the face of his glory. The more that Christians meditate now on this limitless inheritance, the more fruitfully we will live in this present evil age, and the more we will add particular treasures to his glory.

This treasure trove of God's glory has dimensions and details we have yet to ponder. Only an infinite subject can engage our perfected minds for an eternity of time. And the glory of God is that infinite subject. Heaven will consist in one brilliant moment of discovery after another. And that is truly a thrilling prospect! So a great part of our heavenly experience of God's glory will consist in his continual

revelation of his mighty actions throughout history to redeem sinners from every nation on earth.

The End for Which God Created and Redeemed

The book of Revelation makes it plain that heaven will be
illuminated by the glory of God. The new universe "has no
need of sun or moon to shine on it, for the glory of God gives
it light, and its lamp is the Lamb" (Rev. 21:23). The New
Jerusalem is designed to glow with the glory of God, for the
city as a whole and the actual streets of the city are made of
pure gold, like clear glass (vv. 18, 21). This transparent gold
will allow the glory of God to make it radiant, as will the
varied jewels that make up the foundations of the walls and
the pearls that make up the gates—everything in the city will
be illuminated with the glory of God in Christ.

But what is "the glory of God"? It is *the radiant display
of his attributes*. The word *attributes* answers the question,
What is God like? God's attributes include his self-existence,
perfection, holiness, love, omnipotence, omniscience, omni-
presence, justice, mercy, patience, and wrath, among others.
The "radiant display" of these attributes means that they
shine before an audience; they are seen, savored, and celebrated. Sometimes the glory of God is directly connected
with bright light, as when the angel appeared to the shep-
herds to announce the birth of the Savior of the world, and
his radiant light terrified them greatly (Luke 2:9). Sometimes
the glory of God is revealed without any unusual visible
light, as when Jesus died on the cross in an eerie darkness
(Matt. 27:45). Whenever the glory of God shines, some attributes of God are put on display before an audience—angels

and/or humans, those whom God gave the ability to understand him and celebrate him for all he is worth.

This was the end, the reason, for which God created the world. Tragically, Adam led humanity into sin, so that instead of glorifying God, we "worshiped and served the creature rather than the Creator" (Rom. 1:25). Yet despite the devastation of Adam's sin, God's glory has triumphed, displayed in the rescue of a multitude of sinners from every nation and every era. No immense nebula in a distant galaxy, nor stretch of rocky cliffs overlooking the Pacific Ocean, nor salmon making a thousand-mile journey upstream, nor even a heavenly chorus of a hundred million angels brings God more glory than the redemption of the sinners who will stand before his throne in eternity singing his praise.

Past, Present, and Future Glory

When this present age has ended and the new heaven and new earth have come, *at that time* our experience of God's glory will be divided into three categories: God's past glory, God's present glory, and God's future glory. At that time, God's past glory will be revealed in his mighty works throughout the history of the world; God's present glory will be revealed in his face, his throne, his angels, his people, New Jerusalem, and the new heaven and new earth; and God's future glory will be revealed in the unfolding events of life in the new universe.

Of God's future glory in heaven, the Bible says very little. There are indications of the saints ruling over cities, owning property, and doing glorious works. Revelation 21:25–26 states that the gates of New Jerusalem will always stand open and the glories of the nations will stream into it, perhaps implying the fruitful labors of our resurrected hands and our perfected minds. Beyond this I do not wish to speculate.

God's present glory in heaven is what most Christians think about when they think about "heaven," the eternal future to which we are all heading. The greatest glory of heaven will be the face of God himself (Rev. 22:4). This "beatific vision" will be the consummation of all heavenly blessedness, joy, and pleasure. Christ will be the greatest display of the glory of God, "the radiance of the glory of God and the exact imprint of his nature" (Heb. 1:3).

However, God will have much glory to show us in his creation as well. The most glorious will be the redeemed themselves, who will "shine like the sun in the kingdom of their Father" (Matt. 13:43). And the new earth will be spectacular, more than present words can describe. We will spend eternity discovering and exploring the staggering beauties of nature in that perfect world. I have seen even in this present cursed world such glories as to take my breath away: the purples and oranges of a sunset over the Grand Canyon; the majestic snow-covered peaks of the Karakoram Mountains in Pakistan; the sun-splashed beauty of a field of wildflowers near the Eiger north face in Switzerland; the deep sound of the wind blowing over the rocky coastline of Acadia National Park in Maine; the rich, musky smell of an old-growth forest in the Blue Ridge Mountains of North Carolina. How much more glorious will be the new earth, liberated at last from its bondage to decay (Rom. 8:21).

The heavenly review of God's past glory is what this book will unfold. For all eternity, God will be unveiling various aspects of the astonishing works he did in this present age.

And though this book is dedicated to our heavenly history lesson, I believe that our experience in heaven will unite all three aspects of God's glory—past, present, and future—in one central theme: the infinite greatness of our triune God!

The Treasures of the Empire Put on Display

The rulers of the earth love to overwhelm visitors to their capital cities through lavish displays of their glory. The wise city plans, grand architecture, wide avenues, museums containing trophies of military conquests in distant lands, beautiful parks, triumphant arches and statues, soaring gilded spires—all proclaim the greatness of the rulers and their empires. This is the way it has been since humans began our history of conquest.

Caesar Augustus boasted, "I found Rome a city of bricks, and left it a city of marble."[1] In 1275, when Marco Polo visited Xanadu, the capital city of Kublai Khan's Mongolian Empire, he was stunned by the size of its assembly hall, which could easily seat six thousand. "Its roof is vermilion, yellow, green, and blue, and the tiles fixed with a varnish so fine that they shine like crystal and can be seen from a great distance."[2] King Solomon's glories so overwhelmed the Queen of Sheba that "there was no more breath in her" (1 Kings 10:5). From his palace roof, King Nebuchadnezzar boasted of his skill as a conqueror, architect, city planner, and visionary leader: "Is this not Babylon the Great that I have built to be a royal residence by my vast power and for my majestic glory?" (Dan. 4:30 CSB). And Persian Emperor Xerxes sumptuously displayed the glories of his empire in Susa for six full months, culminating in a seven-day banquet for his nobles (Esther 1:4–7).

What human rulers have done from vainglory, God will do for the eternal delight of his people. Unlike the brief visit made by the Queen of Sheba or an evening walk on a rooftop palace or even 180 days of feasting, God will place the glories of his kingdom on display for all eternity. And while Caesar chose marble for his majestic structures and Kublai Khan vermilion tiles to decorate his soaring roof, God's chosen medium of his artistry is people, and the rays of his glory will shine in the innumerable powerful works he did to save his chosen people throughout history.

Thousands of Years of Thousands of Years

Who can fully appraise the treasures of God's glory woven into even a single day of history? We all underestimate the value of those treasures! The Bible makes this amazing assertion about time: "With the Lord one day is as a thousand years" (2 Pet. 3:8). It is as though God sees every single second of history in extreme slow motion. Every flap of a hummingbird's wing, every flutter of a leaf in a summer storm, every glance of an eye or gesture of a hand on the entire surface of the earth is intimately studied by God. As Job said, "Does he not see my ways and number all my steps?" (Job 31:4). The activity of any single day is utterly mindboggling: all over the world, human beings are speaking, acting, making choices, creating. And God is there, watching and recording everything.

But Scripture goes beyond a simple assertion of God's presence and awareness. The doctrine of providence teaches that God is acting decisively through the greatest and smallest events to bring about his sovereign purposes. He controls the casting of a lot (Prov. 16:33) and the decisions of a king

(21:1). He oversees the death of a sparrow (Matt. 10:29) and the birth of a mountain goat (Job 39:1). He chooses the time and circumstances of our birth as well as our death, numbering all the days in between (Ps. 139:16). He acts in ways that are incomprehensible to us, and his footsteps cannot be tracked (Rom. 11:33). The daily actions of God are immeasurable and worthy of praise: secretly restraining tyrants, directing the complex flow of international commerce, answering the prayers of a child, protecting persecuted house church leaders, convicting Christians of secret sin, preparing the tribal leader of an unreached people group to come to Christ, orchestrating the initial meeting of a man and woman who will someday be married.

The sovereign salvation plan of God was crafted before the foundation of the world, bought at infinite cost by the blood of his Son, and applied by the Holy Spirit to individuals in every generation and in every corner of the world. Every day, that plan generates unique treasures . . . thousands of years of thousands of years.

How God's Treasures Have Been Lost

But most details of that plan are hidden from human view, forgotten by succeeding generations, lost through the death of eyewitnesses, and buried under the rise and rubble of nations. God is temporarily deprived of the glory he deserves for both his mighty and minute deeds.

The vast majority of God's glorious deeds in history have never been recorded in any book and never will be. They were performed in the obscure lives of people the world would consider unremarkable—"not many of you were wise according to worldly standards, not many were powerful, not many were of noble birth" (1 Cor. 1:26). These ranks of the redeemed received amazing grace poured on them, and their stories are well worth learning to the glory of God. Yet not only are those stories lost to posterity but the full dimensions of God's activities in saving their souls were often veiled from them as well. They never fully realized how God orchestrated providential occurrences in space and time to bring them to faith in Christ and to help them grow in grace after that. But why should God be robbed of his glory by having those works hidden forever, lost in the dust of the past?

Heaven Will Be Dynamic

My conception of heaven is of a dynamic place full of thrilling activity. Glorified people will *grow and develop*. I once thought of glorification as immediate completion in every area of humanity, including knowledge. That would mean it would be impossible for a glorified person to learn anything at all, as if at glorification we receive an instantaneous and infinite download of all possible information and then remain static for all eternity.

We will never be God, not even in glory. So, we will never be omniscient. There will always be something new to learn. But God does not learn. As I've heard one pastor put it, "Has it ever occurred to you that nothing has ever occurred to God?"[3] For all eternity, new things about God's glory will *occur* to us! And that will make heaven a very exciting place.

In his marvelous book *Heaven*, Randy Alcorn opened my eyes to the delights of a dynamic view of heaven.[4] As he was doing research on the topic, he encountered many Christians who were dreading going to heaven. The shabby cartoonish conceptions of heaven poured into them from childhood were hardly appealing: sitting on a cloud forever and ever, strumming a harp, and singing "Amazing Grace" with a heavenly choir. And as the lyrics to that wonderful hymn imply, "When we've been there ten thousand years, bright shining as the sun, we've no less days to sit on this cloud and strum this harp than when we've first begun." Such a static vision of heaven is depressing to many, and with good reason: it seems an eternal existence of suspended animation, frozen in unchanging "perfection."

Recently I read a disturbing article entitled "Ten Reasons Christian Heaven Would Actually Be Hell." It argues that an eternity of unchanging perfection would be depressing:

> Much of what makes life worth living is the process of learning and discovery, growth and change. We delight in novelty and laugh when we are startled by the unexpected. Curiosity is one of our greatest pleasures, and growth is one of our deepest values and satisfactions. . . . By contrast, timeless perfection is static . . . it means there is no room for improvement—for change and growth. Perfection is sterile in every sense of the word.[5]

But if we accept the concept of a continual discovery of the glory of God, then our conception of heaven becomes incredibly appealing. It also helps explain Isaiah 9:7: "Of the *increase* of his government . . . there will be no end." Since there will be no babies born in heaven, this endless increase must consist in an ever-deepening sense of the glories of Christ's kingly reign. If the redeemed will be continually learning new aspects of his glory, and if Christ is appearing increasingly amazing through studying him and his works, then the inhabitants of his kingdom will become wealthier and wiser for all eternity.

Against Heavenly Amnesia

Some immigrants arriving at New York's Ellis Island in the nineteenth century were glad to change their names and sever their cord to the past. Some were running from their actions or from the conditions of the Old World: people seeking to escape justice for their crimes, people stuck in a socio-economic cycle of poverty from which there was no escape, people experiencing a war or famine that drove them to sell everything to buy a one-way ticket to America. And when they disembarked in New York, they were eager to start fresh, with no ties to the past.

In the same way, some Christians look forward to leaving this painful world entirely behind and sailing on to a new shore. They delight in a future world, a fresh start not haunted by their past. They think of the sadness of their lives on earth and ask, "Why wouldn't we desire a completely cleansed memory when we arrive in heaven?" Three categories of painful memories especially seem to beg for heavenly amnesia: our sins, our sufferings, and our loved ones who were condemned to hell. It seems beneficial to reboot the glorified human mind with a completely wiped memory, like the purge done to a smartphone when you sell it—wiped forever of all your data.

But such a comprehensive forgetting would rob God of his glory and our joy in the redemption of his people. Increased heavenly understanding of earthly history will in turn increase our heavenly joy. This eternal education in history will be glorious! We will be so free from selfish concerns for our reputations that we will finally see God at the glorious center of it all—the Redeemer, Protector, Warrior, Ruler, Healer, Feeder, Author, Perfecter—in a word, the Savior worthy of all praise. That's the point of it all, the end for which God both created and redeemed the world.

CHAPTER 2

Biblical Proof
of Heavenly Memories

When we think about heaven, there are two errors that commonly arise. Either we imagine realities about heaven that have no basis in God's Word, or we come far short of God's revelation and do not think much about heaven at all. Both errors lead to hearts starved for eternal hope. For centuries, false religions have led their followers astray with visions of the afterlife: Norse Valhalla, Buddhist Nirvana, Muslim Paradise, Greco-Roman Elysium, and so on. Recently, people who have had near-death experiences (NDEs) on the brink of eternity have relayed vivid dreams and visions of what heaven will be like. These NDEs have offered false hope to many while providing disharmonious and unauthoritative pictures of heaven. Such imaginary visions of heaven are dangerous.

To avoid these fantasies, some Christians veer in the other direction. John Calvin warned against speculating on heaven:

We must all the more, then, keep sobriety, lest forgetful of our limitations we should soar aloft with the greater boldness, and be overcome by the brightness of the heavenly glory. We also feel how we are titillated by an immoderate desire to know more than is lawful. From this, trifling and harmful questions repeatedly flow forth.[1]

While this restraint is sober-minded, it is too restrictive if we fall short of all that God has revealed to us. The truth of what God has prepared for those who love him will never naturally enter the human heart, but "these things God has revealed to us through the Spirit" (1 Cor. 2:10). Our meditation upon the heavenly life should go as far as Scripture and sound theological reasoning permit but no further. So, what does Scripture say about heavenly knowledge of earth's history?

The God of Abraham, Isaac, and Jacob

Jesus's proof of the resurrection from the dead was profound: "Have you not read what was said to you by God: 'I am the God of Abraham, and the God of Isaac, and the God of Jacob'? He is not God of the dead, but of the living" (Matt. 22:31–32). God uses the present tense, saying "I am Abraham's God *right now*! He is still alive, and we continue to have a relationship here in heaven." This proves that we retain in heaven memories of our lives on earth. If Abraham still exists *as Abraham*, his history must remain, or he would lose his identity. If Abraham's memory was completely wiped in heaven, he would no longer be the same man we read about in the Bible. We would know more now about his earthly life than he does.

Jesus said, "Many will come from east and west and recline at table with Abraham, Isaac, and Jacob in the kingdom of heaven" (8:11). If earthly memories evaporate in heaven, those who come from the east and west (gentile converts to Christ) will have no recollection of their own origins, and feasting with Abraham, Isaac, and Jacob will have no particular meaning. Imagine sitting next to Abraham at the heavenly banquet and having no idea who he is. Clearly Jesus anticipates an experience of fellowship among the saints enriched by perfected memories of earthly lives. Without our life stories, we would essentially be clones with meaningless name badges.

Covenantal Promises Finally Fulfilled

If Abraham has no earthly memory, then what could we make of the covenantal promises made by God that Abraham died without receiving? Concerning the promised land, God said to Abraham,

> Lift up your eyes and look from the place where you are, northward and southward and eastward and westward, for all the land that you see I will give to you and to your offspring forever. . . . Arise, walk through the length and the breadth of the land, for I will give it to you. (Gen. 13:14–17)

Abraham died in faith, not having received the things promised (Heb. 11:13). But he saw them from afar, acknowledging that he was an alien and a stranger on earth. He was desiring a better country, a heavenly one (v. 16). The only way God will keep this promise is if the "heavenly country" is the same land resurrected in heavenly glory, like our resurrection bodies—the same but different. So, the new earth must be this present earth raised from corruption to eternal glory. If God gives Abraham a different world (even if it's a better one), he didn't exactly keep the promise made in Genesis 13:14–17. And if God gives him the actual land restored in glory, but Abraham's mind has no memory of the past, how will he and his children rejoice in God's faithfulness in keeping his promise?

An Eternal Display of the Glory of Grace

In Ephesians 2:6–7, Paul celebrates God's grace in the lives of all Christians:

> [God] raised us up with him and seated us with him in the heavenly places in Christ Jesus, so that *in the coming ages* he might show the immeasurable riches of his grace in kindness toward us in Christ Jesus.

The overwhelming riches of God's grace stagger the mind, far above our ability to comprehend. We vastly underestimate this grace. Ephesians 2:7 tells us one day we will see the infinite dimensions of his grace in Christ. Our education in grace has barely begun in our brief time on earth. The phrase "in the coming ages" points to eternity in heaven. It implies an eternal expansion of our understanding of God's grace and kindness to us in Christ.

For Ephesians 2:7 to come true in heaven, we must never lose our sense of being sinners saved by God's grace. This perpetual awareness of our past sinfulness will bring us no pain, no anguish, no regrets, and no shame, for Revelation 21:4 says there will be no death, mourning, crying, or pain in heaven. But a complete memory loss would rob the redeemed of their ability to praise God for his glorious grace. They would be able to sing "Amazing Grace" in heaven, but they could not declare, "I once was lost, but now am found; was blind, but now I see."

Rewards

Scripture is clear that God will give rewards to his servants. Heavenly rewards are eternally connected to earthly deeds and would in fact be meaningless apart from them. They are honors given by the Father for those who are persecuted for the sake of Christ (Matt. 5:11–12); love their enemies at great cost to themselves (v. 46); secretly give to the needy (6:3–4); privately pray to the Father (v. 6); quietly fast (vv. 17–18); materially support those who preach the Word of God (10:41–42); feed the poor, crippled, lame, and blind (Luke 14:13–14); and so on. Behind each reward will be a specific story worth recounting because each tells of the glory of God and of the people of God. Heavenly rewards must be directly connected to earthly deeds or their radiance will be meaningless. In fact, we can say no story, no glory!

Studying the Mighty Deeds of God

God displays his glory through both his majestic person and his mighty deeds. As the psalmist said, "Praise the LORD! Praise God in his sanctuary; praise him in his mighty heavens! Praise him *for his mighty deeds*; praise him *according to his excellent greatness!*" (Ps. 150:1–2). Looking on the face of almighty God will give us the greatest sense of his excellence. But the psalmist is clear that God's "mighty deeds" are worthy of praise as well, especially in "his mighty heavens." God displays his nature in his powerful actions in history. Repeatedly, the Psalms recount God's mighty deeds as the basis of their praise.

> Great are the works of the LORD,
> *studied by all who delight in them.*
> Full of splendor and majesty is his work,
> and his righteousness endures forever.
> He has caused his wondrous works to be remembered;
> the LORD is gracious and merciful. (111:2–4)

I love this passage! If the great works of the Lord are worthy to be studied now, how much more in heaven? With God as our history teacher, how sweet will be the lessons of God's mighty works for a perfectly prepared audience of the redeemed? That Psalm 111:3 says God's righteous works will endure *forever* is strong evidence of heavenly memory of God's amazing achievements on earth. He will be as worthy of praise for the Red Sea crossing in eternity as he is right now. God's works will never perish, spoil, or fade, because he himself is immutable—he is the same yesterday, today, and forever.

God will delight to bring out those "old treasures" of his glory and display them for his redeemed (Matt. 13:52). If a collector purchases a costly and rare treasure, like a Rembrandt painting, a DaVinci notebook, or a first edition King James Bible, would he or she not greatly delight in bringing it out to show dinner guests? So God uses "display" language for the treasures of his glory in history. He will invite us, his honored guests, to look on each one in turn. *"Come and see what God has done*: he is awesome in his deeds toward the children of man" (Ps. 66:5). In heaven, God will point to each glorious moment in history: "Have you considered this? Come, behold my glory in that unique instance . . . study it, let the light hit it from different angles until you see how I displayed my power, my justice, my compassion, my wisdom, my grace in that unique circumstance."

The Great Congregation

The Psalms celebrate the mighty deeds of God in "the great congregation." God has made clear that his worship is multiplied when enjoyed among his people. So, he ordained that three times a year, the nation of Israel would assemble at the central place of his choosing (Deut. 16:16–17). The people were commanded to bring an offering in proportion to how the Lord had blessed them. No one was to appear empty-handed, without a physical sacrifice from the flocks or herds or fruits of the land. In the Psalms, offerings would also include words of praise from specific Israelites among "the great congregation."

> I will tell of your name to my brothers;
>> in the midst of the congregation I will praise you:
> You who fear the LORD, praise him!
>> All you offspring of Jacob, glorify him,
>> and stand in awe of him, all you offspring of
>>> Israel! . . .

> From you comes my praise in the great congregation;
> my vows I will perform before those who fear
> him. (Ps. 22:22–25)

The redeemed of the Lord will delight in sharing among the assembly of God's people the mighty works he has done in their lives. In fact, Psalm 111, which we just mentioned, is set in the context of the "congregation":

> Praise the LORD!
> I will give thanks to the LORD with my whole heart,
> *in the company of the upright, in the*
> *congregation.*
> Great are the works of the LORD,
> studied by all who delight in them.
> Full of splendor and majesty is his work,
> and his righteousness endures forever.
> He has caused his wondrous works to be remembered;
> the LORD is gracious and merciful. (vv. 1–4)

Hebrews 12 depicts the heavenly Zion this same way:

> You have come to Mount Zion and to the city of the living God, the heavenly Jerusalem, and to *innumerable angels in festal gathering*, and to *the assembly of the firstborn* who are enrolled in heaven, and to God, the judge of all, and to the spirits of the righteous made perfect. (vv. 22–23)

Why would God command Israel to assemble for praise and predict that there will be a similar heavenly assembly but then decree that his mighty deeds for his people be forgotten in heaven?

The Wounds, Works, and Words of the Lamb of God

The glorified Jesus Christ will be the focus of heavenly worship. In Revelation 5, he is celebrated as the triumphant "Lion of the tribe of Judah" and portrayed as a "Lamb standing, as though it had been slain" (vv. 5–6). His mighty accomplishments at the cross and the empty tomb are not forgotten but eternally remembered and adored by the heavenly host.

> And they sang a new song, saying,
>
> > "Worthy are you to take the scroll
> > > and to open its seals,
> > *for you were slain*, and *by your blood you ransomed*
> > > *people for God*
> > > from every tribe and language and people and
> > > > nation,
> > and you have made them a kingdom and priests to
> > > our God,
> > > and they shall reign on the earth." (vv. 9–10)

This single passage confirms that Christ's work of redemption will be remembered and celebrated for all eternity. His resurrected body retains the wounds from the cross—nail marks in his hands, the spear mark in his side (John 20:20, 27).

Christ's heavenly wounds indicate that the full complement of Christ's works will be seen for all eternity. John acknowledged that a complete record of Christ's life was impossible for him: "I suppose that the world itself could not contain the books that would be written" (21:25). But eternity will be long enough to study *all* of Jesus's words and works—not just those recorded in the Gospels!

And finally, Christ's words—every one of them—will endure forever: "Heaven and earth will pass away, but my words will not pass away" (Matt. 24:35). In heaven, we will still know his parables, his Sermon on the Mount, his disputes with his enemies, his extended teachings on himself as the Bread of Life (John 6), the Good Shepherd (John 10), and the Vine (John 15). In heaven, we will see that his Great Commission was completed (Matt. 24:14; 28:19–20). In heaven, we will see that every single one of Christ's sheep were raised up on the last day, just as Jesus said they would be (John 6:39). And not only this, but Jesus's eternally remembered words will be a gateway into all manner of things being remembered in heaven, including Peter's sinful denial and the sufferings of his people at the hands of powerful oppressors.

"In Memory of Her"

Shortly before his death, Mary of Bethany anointed Jesus with an expensive perfume. Speaking to his shocked disciples, Jesus defended her: "Truly, I say to you, wherever this gospel is proclaimed in the whole world, what she has done will also be told in memory of her" (Matt. 26:13). Jesus's words have been fulfilled, as the story of Mary's gift has been told for almost two thousand years. Her pattern of sacrificial love to the Lord stands over all time, challenging every generation of Christians to a similar devotion. Jesus wanted us to remember her . . . and so we do. But why would we stop remembering her once we get to heaven? When we meet Mary in heaven, why would that detail of her life disappear from the collective memories of the redeemed? And since

Jesus's words will never pass away, his statement about her will be remembered forever—as will her act.

But Mary's devotion is just one among countless acts of sacrificial love that have flowed from the hearts of his people. If her act of love is remembered for all eternity, why would other actions of devotion for Jesus be forgotten? They will not!

Thanksgiving Consummated

Refusing to thank God is a great sin: "For although they knew God, they did not honor him as God *or give thanks to him*, but they became futile in their thinking, and their foolish hearts were darkened" (Rom. 1:21). When God converts a sinner, the response is a life of continual thankfulness to God. However, our hearts are still imperfect. We are terribly forgetful and take for granted most of the blessings God lavishes on us every day. When Jesus cleansed ten lepers, only one of them came back to thank him (Luke 17:15–16). Like those nine other lepers, we are often thankless for God's good gifts. So every time we enjoy anything earthly—spectacular scenery, delicious food, fellowship with friends, skillfully played music—we should give thanks, for "every good gift and every perfect gift" is from God (James 1:17).

Heaven is our opportunity to rectify that great wrong—a second chance to give thanks for all the blessings he has lavished on us. Indeed, thanksgiving plays a major role in the heavenly worship in Revelation. And this thankfulness is almost always based on *past* blessings. In Revelation 4, the living creatures "give glory and honor and thanks" to

God, prompting the twenty-four elders to fall on their faces and cast their crowns before God and give thanks to God for creating and sustaining all things (vv. 9–11). The word *whenever* is used, showing a pulsating pattern of repeated thanksgiving for God's past actions.

When God's minute activities in every single day are perfectly revealed, the redeemed in heaven will get to thank God for things he did, even through unbelievers who robbed him of credit. God gave to Cyrus the Great an empire for which he never thanked him (Isa. 45:1–5). Similarly, God has given countless scientists, inventors, composers, artists, writers, and architects insights and concepts and skills that have greatly enriched the world. But most have never given him thanks.

For example, in the early part of the twentieth century, Indian mathematical genius Srinivasa Ramanujan filled three notebooks with 3,900 complex formulas that came to his mind wholly formed but with no proofs. He gave credit to the Hindu goddess Mahalakshmi, saying she revealed scrolls of mathematical formulas before his eyes, and he wrote them down.[2] But heaven will prove these flashes of insight came from the true God. The redeemed in heaven will properly thank God for these revelations. So also for Beethoven's symphonies and Edison's inventions. We will restore to God the glory unbelievers have stolen from him by their thanklessness.

The Stories of the Vast Multitude

One of the most spectacular images of the perfected church in the Bible comes from Revelation 7:

After this I looked, and behold, a great multitude that no one could number, from every nation, from all tribes and peoples and languages, standing before the throne and before the Lamb, clothed in white robes, with palm branches in their hands, and crying out with a loud voice, "Salvation belongs to our God who sits on the throne, and to the Lamb!" (vv. 9–10)

Then comes a question from one of the elders: "These who are clothed in the white robes, *who are they, and where did they come from?*" (v. 13 NASB).

What a key question for this book on heavenly memories! In fact, I suggest the whole concept of this book might begin with this question and its eternally fascinating answer. If there is a complete loss of earthly memory in heaven, answering these questions would be impossible. If God means for us to forget our earthly lives and to experience only the new heaven and new earth, then why would such a question come to the lips of this elder? Obviously, God wants the earthly lives of this vast multitude to be remembered and celebrated, "to the praise of his glorious grace" (Eph. 1:6). They will be trophies of his grace from "every nation, tribe, people, and language." These earthly distinctions will be remembered in heaven so that God's definition of diversity may be celebrated for all eternity. The elect from groups such as the Sawi of Irian Jaya, the Burmese and Karen of Myanmar, the Han of China, and the Huaroni of Ecuador (all converted through the past two centuries of missions) will stand with clear emblems and marks of their ethnicity and give credit to the same Lord and Savior! A memory of our earthly lives will be essential to this thrilling display of unity amid God-ordained diversity.

The Cry for Vengeance

In Revelation 6, as the Lamb of God breaks open the seven seals, the martyrs under the altar cry out for vengeance against their killers:

> They cried out with a loud voice, "O Sovereign Lord, holy and true, how long before you will judge and avenge our blood on those who dwell on the earth?" Then they were each given a white robe and told to rest a little longer, until the number of their fellow servants and their brothers should be complete, who were to be killed as they themselves had been. (vv. 10–11)

These martyrs in heaven are aware of the suffering of their earthly lives and cry out to the Avenger for a justice that has yet to arrive.

As the events of this present age unfold in the book of Revelation, it is clear that the inhabitants of heaven are aware of current events on earth. They celebrate the purposes of God in judging earth-dwellers and delivering his people. For example, in Revelation 11:16–17, after the seventh angel blows his trumpet, the twenty-four elders fall on their faces and thank God for beginning his powerful reign, having defeated the raging nations. If heaven has real-time awareness of God's work as it develops, how much more will heaven celebrate the fullness of God's mighty works when the story is finally complete? It would be surpassingly strange for heaven-dwellers to celebrate earthly details until the end of this age only to jettison all knowledge of God's achievements in the world to come.

Celebrating Certain Attributes of God

The centerpiece of heavenly joy will be to worship God for his glorious attributes. But many of those attributes are so tied to our present earthly sins and sufferings that, if all memory of our past lives is removed, then our celebration of those attributes will lack all context in heaven and become meaningless. The Lord himself reminds us that he is "merciful and gracious, slow to anger, and abounding in steadfast love and faithfulness" (Exod. 34:6). How will we celebrate these attributes if all memory of our sins and sufferings passes away at death? God never changes; he will remain merciful, gracious, and slow to anger for all eternity. But God's demonstration of those precious attributes will be impossible in a perfect world. We will never suffer again, so we will need no new demonstrations of God's compassion. We will never sin again, so there will be no new ways for God to show us his grace. We will be perfectly conformed to Christ, so God will not have any way to show us afresh that he is a longsuffering, patient God. However, we will rejoice in all of God's attributes forever in heaven because of our eternally glorious backward look at all the ways God displayed each one in this present evil age.

CHAPTER 3

Resurrected Bodies, Minds, and Hearts

On August 21, 2017, a solar eclipse made its way across the southeastern United States. That afternoon some friends and I used special glasses to view it. Even with a 93 percent eclipse, the light was not noticeably reduced—it just seemed like a normal sunny afternoon. A few of us foolishly risked glimpsing the sun unaided (if only for a split second) and instantly regretted it! The brilliance of the sun was absolutely overpowering.

If this is true of our far-off star, how much more overpowering would a full revelation of the glory of God be? When Moses begged of God, "Please show me your glory" (Exod. 33:18), he was asking for the greatest gift God could ever bestow. But that day on Mount Sinai, God could not grant Moses's request, "for no one may see me and live" (v. 20 NIV). God hid Moses in a rock cleft and only allowed him to see his back. Yet Revelation 22:4 tells us that the saints in glory "will see his face, and his name will be on their fore-heads." How can they gaze directly at what no one on earth could survive for an instant? All our senses in this present age can be overwhelmed: light can be blinding and sound can be deafening. How can we see God's full glory and find it delightful rather than deadly?

Prepared for Glory

Jonathan Edwards began a sermon on Elijah's contest with the prophets of Baal with these powerful words: "It is the manner of God, before he bestows any signal mercy on the people, first to prepare them for it."[1] In Romans 9:23, Paul speaks of what God did to "make known the riches of his glory for vessels of mercy, which *he has prepared beforehand for glory.*" Every day, God is shaping his elect like a skillful potter, preparing his creation to *be glory* and *see glory*. God finishes with a flourish, instantly glorifying his people and completely conforming them to Christ in mind, heart, and body (8:29–30). This glorification will enable us to experience the "signal mercy" of God: displaying and delighting in the glory of God in heaven.

The Glorious Resurrection Body

Paul tells us, "Flesh and blood cannot inherit the kingdom of God, nor does the perishable inherit the imperishable" (1 Cor. 15:50). Our present bodies cannot handle the glory that God will pour out on us, so God must transform us radically. He makes this plain by four statements contrasting our mortal bodies with our resurrection bodies:

So is it with the resurrection of the dead. What is sown is perishable; what is raised is imperishable. It is sown in dishonor; it is raised in glory. It is sown in weakness; it is raised in power. It is sown a natural body; it is raised a spiritual body. (vv. 42–44)

Perishable means our bodies on earth are continually decaying and heading toward our destination of death. The buried, rotting corpse is the final proof of that lifelong process. Adam was condemned to sink down into the dust from which he came (Gen. 3:19). Our bodies are in bondage to decay, just like the cursed world around us (Rom. 8:21). *Imperishable* means our resurrection bodies will have no process of decay but will be eternally renewed by the principle of life continually flowing from almighty God. We will never die, so our time there will be limitless. Furthermore, our physical capabilities will in no way diminish as eternity unfolds. In this world, our eyes become dim with age. But our resurrected eyes will forever remain perfectly able to drink in the beauty of New Jerusalem.

Dishonor means that the process of death is repulsive, stripping humanity of its visible dignity. The sights, sounds, and smells of an ICU or a nursing home are all the evidence we need for how dishonored the dying body is. And how much more disgusting is a corpse that has been rotting in the earth or decomposing in the sea! *Glory* captures the radiance of the resurrection body. As Christ said so powerfully, "Then the righteous will shine like the sun in the kingdom of their Father" (Matt. 13:43). Also, Daniel 12:3 says, "Those who are wise shall shine like the brightness of the sky above; and those who turn many to righteousness, like the stars forever and ever." This is what I mean by saying that, in heaven, the redeemed will both *see glory* and *be glory*.

Weakness refers to the body's powerlessness in this world. We get tired easily, need to eat to regain our strength, and will have no power to fight off the disease that finally kills us. No body is weaker than a corpse about to be buried. *Power* will characterize the resurrection body . . . limitless power! That does not necessarily mean we will be like Superman, able to fly or leap tall buildings in a single bound. Rather, like Isaiah 40:31 puts it, "[We] shall run and not be weary, [we] shall walk and not faint."

Natural refers to the body we have known in this present age of disease, pain, and death. *Spiritual* is a word that stretches the imagination to the breaking point when Paul speaks of a "spiritual body." I think Jesus's own amazing resurrection body gives us some sense of what this could mean. He had flesh and bones, could be touched physically, and could eat broiled fish (Luke 24:39–43). But he could also pass through the stone walls of the tomb and through the locked doors of the upper room. He could suddenly disappear, then reappear elsewhere.

So this will be our resurrection body: imperishable, glorious, powerful, and spiritual: a body perfectly prepared for the universe of God's glory we will experience for all eternity!

Massive Strengthening Required

Without this immeasurable resurrection upgrade, we would crumble under the weight of glory that God is planning to lay on us. See how Paul speaks of the strengthening Christians need to handle an increased revelation of God's love even in this world:

> [I pray] that according to the riches of his glory he may grant you to be *strengthened* with power through his Spirit in your inner being, so that Christ may dwell in your hearts through faith—that you, being rooted and grounded in love, may have *strength* to comprehend with all the saints what is the breadth and length and height and depth, and to know the love of Christ that surpasses knowledge, that you may be filled with all the fullness of God. (Eph. 3:16–19)

This "strengthening" language is preparatory to an amazing work of the Spirit within us, a foretaste of Christ's love each of us will experience in heaven. Paul prays for all Christians to be strengthened internally, much like the architectural buttressing that allows the floor of a repository for gold bullion not to collapse under such massive weight. The infinite love of God that the Holy Spirit will pour into our souls is so weighty that we could not handle it without this preparation. So, in verse 18, Paul prays that we would have strength to comprehend what God wants us to comprehend. And what is that? The infinite dimensions of Christ's love for us—their breadth and length and height and depth! Imagine the incalculable distances between the galaxies or the light years between our solar system and even the nearest star. The universe in all its immensity is nothing compared to the boundless love of God in Christ for *all* the saints, *every single one* of his beloved elect. When we grasp this love fully, we will be "filled with all the fullness of God." As full as God is, that is how full all the saints will be in our glorification!

Amazingly, the "strengthening" language here merely mentions *foretastes* of this heavenly fullness. Awesome previews of heaven are occasionally granted to some believers here on earth. Paul was "caught up to the third heaven" and had an experience he could not articulate (2 Cor. 12:2–4). In 1737, Jonathan Edwards was out in the woods praying and had a vision of Christ that left him lying on the ground for over an hour, swimming in tears, "emptied and annihilated."[2] His wife, Sarah, had a similar experience that was even more intense. She felt like a dust speck swimming in a sea of light, pleasure flowing and reflowing through her body: "It seemed to be *all my feeble frame could sustain* of that fullness of joy of those who behold the face of Christ . . . in the heavenly world."[3] God granted evangelist D. L. Moody a vision of heaven so powerful that he "had to ask Him to stay His hand."[4]

Why stop so glorious a sight? Because if any more came upon him, Moody felt he would crumble and break. In the electrical wiring of a house, electricians use circuit breakers to protect the house from the heat that is generated by excessive electrical current. Three space heaters plugged into one outlet would draw such a current and so overheat the wires that the wooden frame of the house would soon be ignited and engulfed in flames. But a circuit breaker will trip and break the flow of current before that happens. God's glory is so much that we humans cannot handle the full experience of it. Without a "circuit breaker," our feeble frame—both mental and physical—would be engulfed, and we would collapse.

We see this in the physical reaction of the godly Daniel to the radiantly brilliant angel who was dispatched from heaven to bring him a prophetic message:

No strength was left in me; my face grew deathly pale, and I was powerless. I heard the words he said, and when I heard them I fell into a deep sleep, with my face to the ground. . . . While he was saying these words to me, I turned my face toward the ground and was speechless. Suddenly one with human likeness touched my lips. I opened my mouth and said to the one standing in front of me, "My lord, because of the vision, anguish overwhelms me and I am powerless. How can someone like me, your servant, speak with someone like you, my lord? Now I have no strength, and there is no breath in me." (Dan. 10:8–9, 15–17 CSB)

Remember, this is Daniel's reaction to an angel, not to God himself. And the angel's remedy at that time shows the perfect strengthening that glorification will give to all the redeemed:

Again the one who looked like a man touched me and gave me strength. "Do not be afraid, you who are highly esteemed," he said. "Peace! Be strong now; be strong." When he spoke to me, I was strengthened and said, "Speak, my lord, since you have given me strength." (vv. 18–19 NIV)

By the strengthening of glorification, we will be able to receive the eternal revelation of God's full glory without being consumed.

Resurrected Minds and Hearts, Not Just Bodies

Glorification will also complete the radical transformation of our thoughts and affections. We may wonder how an eternal education could be pleasing to us, but glorification will

47

eternally eliminate the corruptions that presently hinder us, such as idolatry, pride, weariness, dullness, and forgetfulness.

Idolatry. As God unfolds redemptive history in heaven, we will see his glory in everything. Yet we will not idolize the heroes and heroines of this glorious story. We will study the men and women of whom the world was not worthy (Heb. 11:38) and see their valor, wisdom, love, and achievement, yet still not fall down before them in worship. Cornelius fell down before Peter, who immediately rebuked him, saying, "Stand up; I too am a man" (Acts 10:26). In heaven we will fully realize this truth: "neither he who plants nor he who waters is anything, but only God who gives the growth" (1 Cor. 3:7). Our souls will be radically God-centered and Christ-centered as every act of history will ultimately display the greatness of God and his Son.

Pride. From infancy, we are fanatically self-interested. In his *Confessions*, Augustine details the sins of self-interest he committed even as a newborn infant, howling and demanding food regardless of the circumstances of his mother.[5] Pride returns every topic to ourselves—what does this say about *me*? We scream for attention. If we achieve anything for God, we demand to be noticed and celebrated. If we are ignored, our flesh howls. If we see others honored, we are jealous and enraged. Joseph's brothers burned with envy when they saw their father bestow the many-colored robe on him. They "hated him and could not speak to him on friendly terms" (Gen. 37:4 NASB).

In heaven, we will see lavish honors heaped on others. But we will be delivered from jealousy and will truly celebrate those honors as though they were our own. The unity of the body of Christ will be fulfilled: "If one member is honored, all rejoice together" (1 Cor. 12:26). This glorified perspective will enable us to be enthralled by other people's stories, no matter how obscure or ordinary those stories might seem. As we see God at work in those stories, we will *lose ourselves* in those glorious scenic vistas. Imagine standing at the Grand Canyon at sunset but being unable to tear your eyes away from your own reflection in a mirror. How disgusting is our pride! But we will be delivered from self-love by God's love. As John Piper said, "Do you feel more loved by God because he makes much of you, or because he frees you to make much of him?"[6]

Weariness. Just as our resurrection body will be tireless, so will our minds and hearts. The Psalms speak of weariness of soul and mind, and Jesus's disciples fell on the ground in Gethsemane "exhausted from their grief" (Luke 22:45 CSB). Mental exertion can make us exhausted. As the Preacher said, "There is no end to the making of many books, and much study wearies the body" (Eccles. 12:12 CSB). God's history course will last for all eternity. But we will never grow weary of these endless lessons! These thrilling revelations will be matched by our undiminished mental energy. We will have glorified attention spans. Like the two disciples with the resurrected Jesus on the Emmaus road, we will say to one another, "Were not our hearts burning within us while he was explaining history to us?" (see Luke 24:32).

Dullness. Jesus rebuked his disciples for their inability to comprehend his teachings, asking "Are you still so dull?" (Matt. 15:16 NIV). In this world, we often do not understand when people try to explain hard things to us. How then can we imagine being able to take in thousands of years of redemptive history, with all the details, personalities, motives, themes, and causes and effects, and make any sense of it at all? But again, we must realize how radically transformed our minds will be in heaven, perfectly able to comprehend. After his resurrection, Jesus "opened [the disciples'] minds to understand the Scriptures" (Luke 24:45). What he begins in us now by the Spirit, he will perfect in our resurrected minds.

Not only will our mental dullness be gone but our heart reactions will be perfect as well. We will no longer be dull emotionally. We will fervently love the things of God, both great and small. We will not shrug and turn away from some detail of redemptive history with boredom and say, "So what?" Our hearts will *burn within us* . . . burning with love for God and for our brothers and sisters. Powerful emotional displays will characterize heavenly worship: "Clap your hands, all peoples! Shout to God with loud songs of joy!" (Ps. 47:1). In heaven, we will see the great moments of redemptive history for what they are: worthy of eternal celebration that God has redeemed this one or that one.

Jesus's parables of Luke 15—the lost sheep, the lost coin, and the prodigal son—show us how much joy the Father has in saving lost sinners and how much he wants others to share the celebration: "Rejoice with me, for I have found my sheep/coin/son that was lost" (v. 6). Jesus said there will be joy in heaven over one sinner who repents (vv. 7, 10). I always thought that the festivities only happened in heaven at the moment of conversion. But what if these conversions are replayed in eternity so that we can continually celebrate with the Father in his salvation of sinners, even one at a time, even one saved a thousand years ago?

Forgetfulness. Sometimes our education can seem pointless because we can scarcely remember the things we have studied. In heaven, we will be healed from our forgetfulness. We will be able to retain the things we learn and so see the limitless glory of God in redemptive history. This is quite a staggering thought, that our resurrected minds will be transformed into ever-increasing storehouses of the great deeds of God throughout the nations and throughout thousands of years.

The Limits to Our Perfection

Now that we have asserted the glories of our resurrected minds, we must establish boundaries. Our minds and hearts will be perfect, yes, but we will not become deities. God alone is omniscient. As we said, nothing new has ever occurred to God. We will never arrive there! New things will continually occur to us as we are perpetually learning. However, we will continue to think in a linear fashion: first A, then B, then C. That is what Christ means by "I am the Alpha and the Omega, the first and the last, the beginning and the end" (Rev. 22:13). History unfolds in linear fashion because that is how humans are built. God alone can think of everything at once. This is part of his infinite mind, his omniscience.

Furthermore, our perfect memories will not allow everything to be on the desktop of our minds at every moment. We will only be able to focus on a limited number of things at once. Charles Spurgeon once said he was conscious of seven different trains of thought going through his mind at one time while preaching.[7] Perhaps we will have that kind of increased capacity, but not infinitely so. Some things will be more in the background, other things front and center. That is why the inhabitants of heaven are *reacting* as things happen in the book of Revelation. For example, when Jesus opened the seventh seal, there was silence in heaven for half an hour (Rev. 8:1). Thus, heavenly worship will have ripples and pulses of reactions as new things are unveiled. Throughout eternity the past will be revealed, and we will celebrate perfectly.

CHAPTER 4

Better Than Virtual Reality

One of the most remarkable developments of our modern age is computer-generated virtual reality (VR), an experience so realistic it causes hearts to race and sweat to form. Military VR trains fighter pilots for extremely dangerous situations without risk to the pilots or the pricey jets. Consumer versions focus primarily on gaming. Goggles and digital gloves track gamers' movements and allow them to interact in scenarios that feel surprisingly real.

But this is only the early stage of VR. In the future, people's artificial existence may allow them to go on some exotic vacation, meet a famous person, or sail on a yacht. Even the sky isn't the limit! Educators could use VR to teach with vivid intensity what it was like to be a soldier fighting in the battle of Gettysburg or to walk on the moon with Neil Armstrong. Though VR-related ethical issues fill me with a sense of foreboding (Satan corrupting souls with the "lusts of the eye"), the power of such visual images cannot be denied.

Journalist Jake Swearingen was blown away by his initial experience with VR:

> I put the helmet on my head and found myself standing on the deck of a sunken ship, the surface of the ocean glittering over my head like the roof of a cathedral as a blue whale glided above me, covering me in shadow. I had a sense of awe, of being very tiny in the presence of something very large, and the very clear thought: *I could live here.*[1]

It is understandable that a *visual* experience could be so moving. On average, 83 percent of our information about the surrounding world comes through eyesight, while only 11 percent comes through hearing, 3.5 percent through smell, 1.5 percent through touch, and 1 percent through taste.[2] Jesus said, "The eye is the lamp of the body. So, if your eye is healthy, your whole body will be full of light" (Matt. 6:22). In heaven, our eyes will perfectly fill our resurrected bodies with the light of God's glory. Some of that glory will shine from God's mighty deeds in the past. And what virtual reality technology can do, God can do infinitely better, with no sweaty helmets, motion sickness, or tired eyeballs.

Heaven: Seeing Is Better Than Hearing

In this age, God has decreed that sinners would be justified by faith (Rom. 3:26), and that faith would come by *hearing* the Word, not by seeing (10:17). We walk by faith, not by sight (2 Cor. 5:7). Faith itself is the "assurance of things hoped for, the conviction of things *not seen*" (Heb. 11:1). But in heaven, our faith will at last become sight. Job asserts that seeing God is better than hearing about him: "I had heard of you by the hearing of the ear, but now my eye sees you" (Job 42:5). Paul predicted a similar transition in the mode of divine communication.

> As for prophecies, they will pass away; as for tongues, they will cease; as for knowledge, it will pass away. For we know in part and we prophesy in part, but when the perfect comes, the partial will pass away. When I was a child, I spoke like a child, I thought like a child, I reasoned like a child. When I became a man, I gave up childish ways. (1 Cor. 13:8–11)

Seeing God and all spiritual realities face-to-face will be infinitely better than hearing these truths in nouns, verbs, adjectives, and adverbs.

> For now we see in a mirror dimly, but then *face to face*. Now I know in part; then I shall know fully, even as I have been fully known. (v. 12)

Seeing Christ with our own eyes will transform us. "When he appears we shall be like him, because we shall see him as he is" (1 John 3:2). It is *because we shall see him* that we will be perfectly conformed to his image. So heaven is all about seeing and not merely hearing. Could the same be true for learning the manifold glories of God woven throughout the tapestry of redemptive history?

Seeing God's Past Grace for All Eternity

The most glorious thing God has ever done is to redeem sinners by his grace and perfect them for heaven by the shed blood of Christ. Ephesians 1 says three times that God did it all for "the praise of his glorious grace." The details of how God did this will be the centerpiece of the backward look at history we will enjoy for all eternity.

> [God] made us alive together with Christ—by grace you have been saved—and raised us up with him and seated us with him in the heavenly places in Christ Jesus, so that *in the coming ages he might show the immeasurable riches of his grace* in kindness toward us in Christ Jesus. (Eph. 2:5–7)

The common use of the Greek word translated "show" is of a *visual* demonstration, lived out before witnesses. "In the coming ages" (for all eternity), God will *show* us how infinitely gracious he was throughout earth's history.

Time Travelers?

How would this be possible? The past is the past; our lives are "a mist that appears for a little time and then vanishes" (James 4:14). If the past is gone so quickly, how could we immerse ourselves in it and wring from those former days all the lessons of God's glory woven into each moment? Would this require time travel? Time travel has always captivated the minds of the imaginative. In Charles Dickens's classic *A Christmas Carol*, the "ghost of Christmas past" uses a vision to take Ebenezer Scrooge back in time to see his childhood:

> They walked along the road, Scrooge recognizing every gate, and post, and tree; until a little market-town appeared in the

distance, with its bridge, its church, and winding river. Some shaggy ponies now were seen trotting towards them with boys upon their backs, who called to other boys in country gigs and carts, driven by farmers. All these boys were in great spirits, and shouted to each other, until the broad fields were so full of merry music, that the crisp air laughed to hear it.[3]

Fiction writers often employ this technique of time travel. Ray Bradbury's 1952 short story "A Sound of Thunder" probes the philosophical conundrums of time travel by relating the devastating effects of the accidental death of a single butterfly trampled by a time-traveling hunter. The 1985 movie *Back to the Future* addresses the same puzzle, as teenager Marty McFly travels back to 1955 only to discover that he's altered the way his parents met and jeopardized his own existence.

However, Christians rightly reject the concept of actual time travel, embracing the linear view of history asserted by Christ: "I am the Alpha and the Omega, the first and the last, the beginning and the end" (Rev. 22:13). There are not infinite parallel universes running simultaneously to which we can be transported. So, *no* . . . we are not advocating actual time travel in heaven!

Visionary Travel by the Prophets

This does not mean that God cannot show us *visions of the past* with such vivid power that we feel we are living through it. And Scripture reveals that such visionary travel has happened before, as Paul describes:

I know a man in Christ who fourteen years ago was caught up to the third heaven—*whether in the body or out of the body I do not know*, God knows. And I know that this man was caught up into paradise—whether in the body or out of the body I do not know, God knows. (2 Cor. 12:2–3)

This vision was so realistic Paul could not tell whether or not he was physically transported to paradise.

The prophet Ezekiel had similar visions in his day, when God took him on a tour of the temple area to show him the wicked acts the Jewish people were doing in secret.

He put out the form of a hand and took me by a lock of my head, and the Spirit lifted me up between earth and heaven and brought me in visions of God to Jerusalem, to the entrance of the gateway of the inner court that faces north. . . .

And he brought me to the entrance of the court, and when I looked, behold, there was a hole in the wall. Then he said to me, "Son of man, dig in the wall." So I dug in the wall, and behold, there was an entrance. And he said to me, "Go in, and see the vile abominations that they are committing here." So I went in and saw. And there, engraved on the wall all around, was every form of creeping things and loathsome beasts, and all the idols of the house of Israel. (Ezek. 8:3, 7–10)

Though Ezekiel was not physically transported to the secret rooms of the temple, he was active in the vision, digging through a wall and learning about the wickedness of Israel. It was a participatory vision. That is a fascinating possibility of how we may view thousands of years of earth's history in heaven.

John was transported by the Spirit to see the coming New Jerusalem:

> [An angel said,] "Come, I will show you the Bride, the wife of the Lamb." And he carried me away in the Spirit to a great, high mountain, and showed me the holy city Jerusalem coming down out of heaven from God, having the glory of God, its radiance like a most rare jewel, like a jasper, clear as crystal. (Rev. 21:9–11)

"He carried me away in the Spirit" is the essence of the visionary time travel we may experience. If John could be transported by the Spirit ahead in time to see the church in all her future glory, why could God not enable all his people to travel back in time to see how the New Jerusalem is constructed, living stone by living stone, from every tribe, language, people, and nation? Now, I must say there is no scriptural assertion that this will happen; I am only saying it *may* happen. God may well have some other way of revealing history to us. But heaven is about seeing, not merely hearing. The heavenly review of history will be more than merely a series of verbal testimonies for all eternity.

So, What Would It Be Like?

Every aspect of human history would be available for God to display to his redeemed. How exciting it would be to see the days of creation replayed. Or to see the construction of Noah's ark, or to be with him and his family on the ark with all those animals. Or to pass through the Red Sea with the Hebrews, led by the pillar of fire. Or to stand with the eyewitnesses of the death of Christ and see the realities of that day accurately replayed by visions from God.

And the visions would go beyond biblical history. Imagine seeing Nestorian missionaries take the gospel to China. Or hearing the powerful, passionate preaching of the new birth by George Whitefield to the coal miners of Bristol. Or being with Billy Graham as he preached to ten thousand in Times Square. Perhaps we might want to know something never recorded on any pages of history, like what happened to the daughter of the Syro-Phoenician woman in Tyre whom Jesus healed from demon-possession. Revelations of the glories of God in every day of redemptive history await us in heaven, and if God chooses, he can display them with visionary vividness.

CHAPTER 5

Rewards

Unequal Capacities for Heavenly Glory

The movie *Patton*, based on the life of General George Patton, ends with the flamboyant WWII general speaking these words:

> For over a thousand years, Roman conquerors returning from the wars enjoyed the honor of a *triumph*, a tumultuous parade. In the procession came trumpeters and musicians and strange animals from the conquered territories, together with carts laden with treasure and captured armaments. The conqueror rode in a triumphal chariot, the dazed prisoners walking in chains before him. . . . But a slave stood behind the conqueror, holding a golden crown and whispering in his ear a warning: "All glory is fleeting!"[1]

Ironically, General Patton's own glory would prove extremely fleeting. He was relieved of his command and soon after died in a tragic road accident in December 1945. The

Roman slave spoke the truth, just as Isaiah said: "All flesh is grass, and all its glory is like the flower of the field. The grass withers, the flower fades" (Isa. 40:6–7).

Yet as transient as earthly glory is, heavenly glory is eternal. And the crowns of honor God will bestow on his faithful servants will never lose their luster. Their rewards will shine undimmed for all eternity.

Squeamishness about Rewards

Many Christians are squeamish about the topic of rewards. Perhaps this comes from the deplorable pride that accompanies most honors given in this world. This pride is inherently self-seeking, for our flesh yearns to make a name for ourselves. We know that Christians should seek that God and God alone be glorified: "Not to us, O LORD, not to us but to your name give glory" (Ps. 115:1). As Keith Green put it, "And when I'm doing well, help me to never seek a crown, for my reward is giving glory to you."[2] However, the scriptural teaching about rewards should drive out our concerns about pride as we understand what heavenly rewards really are, and how saturated in the glory of God they will be.

God Will Reward His Servants

The Bible teaches that God will reward his servants for works they have done on earth. In his Sermon on the Mount, Jesus encourages three good works: giving money to the needy, praying, and fasting. For all three, he urges his disciples to do them in secret so that their Father, "who sees what is done in secret," will reward them (Matt. 6:4, 6, 18 NASB). He then gives this powerful conclusion:

Do not store up for yourselves treasures on earth, where moth and rust destroy, and where thieves break in and steal. But *store up for yourselves treasures in heaven*, where neither moth nor rust destroys, and where thieves do not break in or steal; for where your treasure is, there your heart will be also. (Matt. 6:19–21 NASB)

The command to store up treasure in heaven cannot refer to good works done before conversion, for the only thing that unregenerate people are storing up by their works is the wrath of God (Rom. 2:5). And since we are justified by faith alone apart from works (3:28), this "storing up" of good works cannot refer to earning our salvation. Therefore, the treasures we are storing up in heaven are rewards for works done after conversion.

In the same way, 1 Corinthians 3 gives strong proof of rewards given on judgment day:

Now if anyone builds on the foundation with gold, silver, precious stones, wood, hay, straw—each one's work will become manifest, for the Day will disclose it, because it will be revealed by fire, and the fire will test what sort of work each one has done. If the work that anyone has built on the foundation survives, *he will receive a reward*. If anyone's work is burned up, he will suffer loss, though he himself will be saved, but only as through fire. (vv. 12–15)

The "gold, silver, [and] precious stones" refer to various levels of quality in work done in building up the "holy temple," which is the church (Eph. 2:20–22). The "wood, hay, [and] straw" refer to any works Christians do that are not worthy of reward. The fire represents God's actions on judgment day in either purifying our good works or destroying our worthless works. But there is no doubt that this passage teaches the reality of rewards in heaven tied directly to our actions on earth. The lasting challenge is to maximize our gold, silver, and costly stones, and to minimize our wood, hay, and straw.

Required to Believe in Rewards . . . and to Seek Them

The book of Hebrews asserts that it is essential to believe that God rewards us, and that we should be zealously looking forward to his rewards at every moment: "And without faith it is impossible to please him, for whoever would draw near to God must believe that he exists *and that he rewards* those who seek him" (Heb. 11:6). Putting it another way, it is impossible to please God if we don't believe that he rewards people who seek him. This statement is toward the beginning of a marvelous chapter, sometimes called the "Hall of Faith," in which great men and women of God are put on display for their acts of faith. One of those great heroes of faith is Moses:

> By faith Moses, when he was grown up, refused to be called the son of Pharaoh's daughter, choosing rather to be mistreated with the people of God than to enjoy the fleeting pleasures of sin. He considered the reproach of Christ greater wealth than the treasures of Egypt, for *he was looking to the reward*. (vv. 24–26)

It was because he wanted an eternal reward that Moses turned his back on a life of worldly pleasures. A continual focus on heavenly reward for earthly sacrifices is not only acceptable but essential to a life that pleases God. Looking ahead to heavenly rewards is not a guilty pleasure for Christians; it is what the life of faith is all about.

Paul Fully Expected His Rewards in the Next Life

Undoubtedly the apostle Paul was mindful of his heavenly rewards during his great suffering. Probably no one in the history of the church endured as many afflictions and such prolonged suffering for the gospel as he. His astonishing catalog of sufferings is recorded for us in 2 Corinthians 11: eight savage beatings, one stoning, three shipwrecks, and continual attacks from his own fellow Jews and from highway robbers. Paul survived three riots caused by his enemies, was in prison countless times, and lived a life of physical privation. "Rejoice and be glad," Jesus said to those persecuted for his name's sake, and he promised, "your reward is great in heaven" (Matt. 5:12). Paul's life of service to Christ resulted in so much suffering that he considered himself the most pitiable man on earth if there is no resurrection from the dead (1 Cor. 15:19). He knew that God was able to guard his precious store of good works that he had entrusted to him for the day of judgment (2 Tim. 1:12).

Crowns in Which We Will Glory

Crowns awarded to servants of the Lord will be the honor and glory of those servants in heaven. Sometimes crowns simply represent the honor of salvation itself (James 1:12; 2 Tim. 4:8). But other crowns are tied to our works on earth. Paul compares his evangelistic efforts to an athlete seeking to win a crown. He strove to become "all things to all people, that by all means I might save some" (1 Cor. 9:22). He was extremely strict in his lifestyle, disciplining his body like an athlete so he would not be disqualified for the crown he was zealous to win (v. 27). However, his goals were unlike those athletes: "They do it to receive a perishable wreath, but we an imperishable" (v. 25). Paul's eye was always on the future glory that would come to him as a result of his zealous efforts. He referred to the Thessalonian Christians as his hope, joy, and crown "of boasting before our Lord Jesus at his coming" (1 Thess. 2:19).

The saints will rule with Christ (Dan. 7:27; 2 Tim. 2:12; Rev. 3:21). However, there is special authority granted to a select few. In Revelation 4, the twenty-four elders are clothed in white, seated on thrones, and wearing golden crowns. Their thrones and crowns represent their rule under the ultimate government of the King of kings. They are honored, sitting in close proximity to the throne of God (Rev. 4:4). Jesus alludes to the privileged few (Matt. 20:20–23) who would sit at his right and his left in the kingdom of heaven. James and John sought those places of honor. But Jesus said that they belonged to those whom the Father prepared them for. Jesus then went on to instruct his disciples on how such places of honor would be granted (vv. 25–28).

What God Will Reward

So, what does the Bible reveal that God will reward for all eternity? Let's walk through some of the various categories.

1. *Anything done for the glory of God (even simple daily tasks).* "So, whether you eat or drink, or whatever you do,

do all to the glory of God" (1 Cor. 10:31). To do something "to the glory of God" means to put him on display before a watching world, even in the most menial actions of life.

2. Humble servanthood. Jesus said, "Whoever would be great among you must be your servant, and whoever would be first among you must be your slave, even as the Son of Man came not to be served but to serve, and to give his life as a ransom for many" (Matt. 20:26–28). Every act of humble servanthood toward others will never lose its reward.

3. Sacrificial giving. The Old Testament sacrificial system was based on something costly given up for God and others. David said, "I will not offer burnt offerings to the Lord my God that cost me nothing" (2 Sam. 24:24). The more something cost us on earth (whether time, energy, money, or other), the greater the reward in heaven. Yet even a small gift, like the widow's two copper coins, can be more valuable than another's gift because sacrifice is measured proportionally (Luke 21:3).

4. Suffering for the kingdom. No sacrifice is greater than one's own life laid down for others (John 15:13), so the martyrs who die for the kingdom give more than anyone else. Similarly, people who suffer pain physically or emotionally for the kingdom will be rewarded in proportion to their suffering (Matt. 5:11–12). When James and John seek the place of honor, the first thing Jesus asks them is, "Are you able to drink the cup that I am to drink?" (20:22). That was the cup of suffering on the cross. Positions of honor are given in his kingdom based on the degree to which people suffer for Christ's name's sake.

5. Advancing the gospel. Other people won to Christ are "[crowns] in which we will glory" in heaven (1 Thess. 2:19

NIV). Any soul-winning effort is rewarded in heaven, but those who venture forth boldly in some courageous pattern of missionary work are especially honored. Paul said, "I *make it my ambition* to preach the gospel, not where Christ has already been named . . . but as it is written, 'Those who have never been told of him will see, and those who have never heard will understand'" (Rom. 15:20–21). Paul's word translated "ambition" literally means "love of honor." Paul yearned for the *honor* of going into an unreached region of the world, to pioneer the church of Christ. This reminds me of David's "mighty men," warriors who vied for the honor of doing great deeds of valor on the battlefield (2 Sam. 23:8–39). How much more will a missionary pioneer who ventured forth into a hostile land for the gospel of Christ be honored!

6. *Giving to the poor.* Jesus said people who feed the poor in this world will be "repaid at the resurrection of the righteous" (Luke 14:14 NIV). We should seek out people who cannot repay us in this world, as though there is a heavenly ledger with "debts outstanding" that God will not fail to repay in heaven.

7. *Secret acts of piety: fasting and prayer.* When we go into a room, close the door, and pray to our unseen Father, he sees what is done in secret and will reward it. So it will be with private acts of fasting or self-denial done for the glory of God (Matt. 6:6, 18). In this way, quietly faithful servants have stored up vast quantities of treasure in heaven.

8. *Anything done to help those advancing the gospel.* This is the "cup of cold water" teaching in Matthew 10:42. Jesus said that anyone who supports gospel workers will receive the same reward as those who do the actual preaching.

9. *Anything done to help other Christians in any way.* Hebrews 6:10 says, "God is not unjust so as to overlook your work and the love that you have shown for his name in *serving the saints,* as you still do." This is the reward of godly widows who "washed the feet of the saints" (1 Tim. 5:10). And it is the framework of the judgment day "sheep and goats" teaching of Jesus in Matthew 25: "Whatever you did for one of the least of these brothers and sisters of mine, you did for me" (v. 40 NIV). Included are works of love such as those of Dorcas, who made robes and other garments for Christians (Acts 9:39).

10. *An honorable life of hard work.* Paul uses the same word as in Romans 15:20, translated "ambition" or "love of honor," in 1 Thessalonians 4:11–12 for the ordinary lives of Christians all over the world: "Make it your ambition to lead a quiet life and attend to your own business and work with your hands, just as we instructed you, so that you will behave properly toward outsiders and not be in any need" (NASB). Christians who work at a job to earn enough money to feed, clothe, and house their family, who conduct their affairs with dignity, and who shine the light of Christ whenever they can will have an eternal reward in heaven. That is the honor we should seek, and it will never be taken from us.

The Reward: Personalized Heavenly Experience of God

If we have any discomfort when contemplating heavenly rewards and honors, it should melt away with this consideration: the essence of the rewards and honors is *God himself.* God is the essence of heaven, for that is what it means when we say that the new heaven, new earth, and New Jerusalem are all completely illuminated by the glory of God. Psalm 16 asserts that resurrection joy will consist of the presence of God: "In your presence there is fullness of joy; at your right hand are pleasures forevermore" (v. 11). Paul traded everything of worth and value in this world—money, power, worldly honors—for one thing: "the surpassing worth" of knowing Christ. Everything else was as rubbish to him (Phil. 3:8–10). And though Paul knew Christ well, he also knew he was just beginning his journey of discovery. For "in [Christ] are hidden all the treasures of wisdom and knowledge" (Col. 2:3). That is why Paul said, "For me to live is Christ, and to die is gain" (Phil. 1:21). That would be blasphemous if he meant "For me to live is Christ, and to die is something better than Christ." But death is a gateway into infinitely increasing knowledge of Christ: "To live is Christ, and to die is *more Christ*!" Jesus said to his heavenly Father, "This is eternal life, that they know you, the only true God, and Jesus Christ whom you have sent" (John 17:3).

Therefore, heaven itself is all about knowing God, for our eternal inheritance is God himself. As he said to Aaron and the Levites, "I am your portion and your inheritance among the Israelites" (Num. 18:20 CSB). Or again, to Abraham, "Fear not, Abram, I am your shield; your reward shall be very great" (Gen. 15:1). The essence of the reward is God, not something other than God. For as Hebrews 11:6 says, we must believe that God exists, and that he rewards those who diligently seek *him*. How could God give something other than himself to people who spent their whole lives diligently seeking him? The reward is in some sense a deeper revelation of God himself. God will give a unique share of himself to each person he desires to honor. It is not idolatrous to seek rewards, because the reward is an extension of seeking God himself.

This will differentiate one redeemed person from another in heaven—an individualized portion of God given to him or her in a way directly tied to that person's life on earth. The heavenly reward is "more of God" than others receive. Therefore, we should think of rewards as varying degrees of capacity for heavenly glory. Perhaps we may think of it as access, proximity, or closeness to God. Although all of the redeemed will see God's face, some will enjoy deeper intimacy with God. I believe all the redeemed in heaven will be perfectly happy, but not all will be equally happy. Rewards are an increased capacity for absorbing and comprehending the glory of God.

Similarly, this reward is an intimate connection between us and our heavenly Father related to specific works we did on earth. God will express a unique pleasure to the son or daughter who did this or that work on earth, speaking words of praise. Of course, heaven will resound with redeemed people and angels giving praise to God, and that will be our greatest delight. But the Bible also speaks of *praise from God*, expressing to us and others how pleased he is with our actions.

> Therefore judge nothing before the appointed time; wait until the Lord comes. He will bring to light what is hidden in darkness and will expose the motives of the heart. At that time each will receive their *praise from God*. (1 Cor. 4:5 NIV)

> [Some] loved human praise more than *praise from God*. (John 12:43 CSB)

On the contrary, a person is a Jew who is one inwardly, and circumcision is of the heart—by the Spirit, not the letter. That person's *praise* is not from people but *from God*. (Rom. 2:29 CSB)

God can and does praise people, and we should earnestly seek the praise he will give us for faithfully serving him. In Jesus's parable of the talents, the master, having entrusted his servants with his property, says to those who were diligent and skillful, "Well done, good and faithful servant. You have been faithful over a little; I will set you over much. Enter into the joy of your master" (Matt. 25:21, 23). This commendation from God should mean everything to us. Any dutiful child constantly seeks to please his or her parent. No one did this more than Jesus, for he said, "I always do what pleases him" (John 8:29 NIV). Our reward is God expressing that pleasure back to his faithful children: "I was so pleased with what you did!" God opens the door of his soul to us so that we might know his heart pleasure over our good deeds ("Enter into the joy of your master"). Heavenly rewards and honors are truly God-centered. They have no existence apart from God. Unlike worldly ambition that drives people to pursue their own glory, holy rewards are all about God expressing personal delight in what we have done.

When we are commanded to give secretly to the needy, not letting our right hand know what our left is doing, we are promised that our Father who sees what is done in secret will reward us (Matt. 6:3–4). How? With a lavish experience of his pleasure in that gift to the poor. He will say, "Let me show you how delighted I was, my child, in that sacrificial act of yours! Enjoy my happiness in that specific moment."

I used to think of "Well done, good and faithful servant" as something God would say once, on judgment day, and never again. Now I realize that God will allow us to relive his pleasure in our specific actions again and again in eternity. Our good deeds will never die but will be rehearsed in heavenly delight forever. There is no limit to how much of this praise we can have from God. Christ commanded us to store up treasure in heaven (v. 21). We can and should store up as much *praise from God* as possible.

Unequal in Glory

There will be distinctions between the redeemed in heaven, as Paul said of the resurrection from the dead, "Star differs from star in glory" (1 Cor. 15:41). The redeemed will all see God's glory (absorb it, take it in, experience it, understand it) but not all will see God's glory equally. Some will have a greater capacity for the infinite glory of God. We will be finite, limited creatures. None of us, no matter how glorious, will be able to comprehend completely the infinite glory of God. But some will have a greater capacity than others.

Think of it like an infinite ocean of glory with a vast number of submerged vessels. The various vessels have larger or smaller dimensions: a thimble, a bucket, a vat, a water tower, an oceangoing supertanker. They are all submerged and 100 percent full, but they have vastly different capacities. So it will be with rewards.

And I believe our earthly lives will determine the size of our heavenly capacity. Jesus reminds us of this reality: "Give, and it will be given to you; a good measure—pressed down, shaken together, and running over—will be poured into your lap. For with the measure you use, it will be measured back to you" (Luke 6:38 CSB). Our rewards for earthly generosity are not of this world; they will be "at the resurrection of the righteous" (14:14 CSB).

Delighting in Each Other's Rewards

The varying levels of reward in heaven will not cause any jealousy or difficulty among the redeemed. As Jonathan Edwards said in his masterpiece "Heaven Is a World of Love," "All shall have as much love as they desire and as great manifestations as they can bear; and so all shall be fully satisfied, and where there is perfect satisfaction, there can be no envy."[3] Imagine heaven as an immense banquet in which there are innumerable dishes, each differently spiced. There is a limitless supply of each dish. Each person at the banquet can eat as much or as little of each dish as they wish. Some like a little of this and a little of that and some of that too; others have a smaller appetite; others like just one dish and eat a lot of it, but there's still plenty of that dish for everyone else. At the end of the meal, after everyone has eaten their fill, there is still plenty of each dish left. How could there possibly be envy or jealousy? In heaven, each will have as much of God as he or she desires.

Furthermore, we will not be jealous of the greater glories and accolades lavished on other Christians in heaven. There are three reasons this is so, according to Edwards:

1) Because the love between the saints will be perfect, and we will truly delight in each other's blessedness:

"There is undoubtedly an inconceivably pure, sweet, and fervent love between the saints in glory . . . without limit or alloy or interruption; and no envy or malice or revenge or contempt or selfishness will ever enter there, but all such feelings will be kept as far away as sin is from holiness and as hell is from heaven."[4]

2) Because we will so completely trust God that we will think any honors he has chosen to give to another are perfectly merited and ultimately display God's glory:

"It will not be a grief to any saint to see another saint elevated and honored above himself."[5]

Actually, the elevation of another will draw forth greater love and admiration and honor, because God has done it and God is revealed and glorified by that person.

3) Because the most glorious will also be the holiest and most aware of their own limitations before the infinite God, they will also be the humblest:

"And there will be no temptation for any to envy those that are above them in glory on account of the latter being lifted up with pride; for there will be no pride in heaven. We are not to conceive that those who are more holy and happy than others in heaven will be elated and lifted up in their spirit above others; for those who are above others in holiness, will be superior to them in humility. The saints that are highest in glory will be the lowest in humbleness of mind, for their superior humility is part of their superior holiness."[6]

"Though all are perfectly free from pride, yet, as some will have greater degrees of divine knowledge than others, and larger capacities to see more of the divine perfections, so they will see more of their own comparative littleness and nothingness, and therefore will be lowest and most abased in humility."[7]

Edwards was merely expanding on what Paul said of the perfect unity of the body of Christ: "If one member is honored, all the members rejoice with it" (1 Cor. 12:26 CSB). In heaven, we will be so delivered from selfishness that we will love to hear the exploits of those greater than ourselves, to learn how God used their extreme devotion and costly sacrifice to establish the kingdom of heaven in the lives of the elect. Their honors will in some sense belong to all of the body.

Casting Our Crowns

Our rewards in heaven will be given solely by grace. Only because Jesus Christ died on the cross for us do we escape the eternal torments of hell. Beyond this, every good work we do in this world, we do by the power of Christ working in us by his Spirit:

Anyone who lives by the truth comes to the light, so that his works may be shown to be *accomplished by God*. (John 3:21 CSB)

I [Jesus] am the vine; you are the branches. Whoever abides in me and I in him, he it is that bears much fruit, for *apart from me you can do nothing*. (15:5)

By the grace of God I [Paul] am what I am, and his grace toward me was not in vain. On the contrary, I worked harder than any of them, though *it was not I, but the grace of God that is with me*. (1 Cor. 15:10)

This is why the twenty-four elders are continually casting their crowns before the throne of God, declaring he alone is worthy of worship (Rev. 4:9–11). Those with thrones and crowns are intensely aware that God's throne is the loftiest; it is only by his grace that they have any honor. All rewards will return to the God who gives all good gifts. "For from him and through him and to him are all things. To him be glory forever" (Rom. 11:36).

CHAPTER 6

God's Sovereign Weaving of the Tapestry of History

Years ago, we visited a high-end Persian rug boutique where the merchant showed us some of the most exquisite works in his collection. The most expensive was a carpet from the 1920s that looked more like a tapestry. He pointed to the details of its craftsmanship so we could see that this was a masterpiece. On the back of the carpet was a dense array of tiny knots, each tied by hand with extreme precision. Only after we saw the back of the carpet did he allow us to see the front, and the effect was breathtaking. Those individual knots, each made of colored silk thread, combined to form the beautiful image of a Persian prince with a long plume in his hat riding a white horse through a mountain pass.[1]

God's heavenly history lesson will be much like this rug. Before the foundation of the world, the Creator wove the entire tapestry of history in his mind: the grand, overarching array of meaning crafted with detail; the overall dimensions measured out; the material, length, and color of every thread; the position of every knot. Then, in a marvelous succession of "todays," God spoke all of it into being. God wove the Alpha and the Omega days, and every day in between. When the redeemed finally get to heaven, God will delight in showing them the magnificent tapestry, unrolling it and lifting it up, pointing to its tiniest details, for the praise of his glory and the delight of his people.

Dimensions and Details

The challenge for us is the impossible combination of *dimensions* and *details*. The dimensions are the overarching story, everything that God will want us to know of millennia of human history. The details are the minute aspects that have gone into every moment. They work together. If in heavenly review we see a huge army flooding through a snowy mountain pass, or two men sitting at a conference table angrily talking over a document, or a woman exulting over something she has just read in a letter, or a small boy cowering in a cave while two men skulk past the entrance . . . none of those moments would mean anything to us without detailed knowledge of the circumstances. But it is of moments like these—various tiny colored knots—that the whole tapestry of God's glory in history is woven.

Peter writes, "With the Lord one day is like a thousand years, and a thousand years like one day" (2 Pet. 3:8 CSB). This one verse gives both sides of the equation. *One day is like a thousand years.* This means even the most mundane, ordinary day of human history contains more information, major occurrences, "random" events, significant conversations, commonplace tasks, devious crimes, sinister plots, and charming moments than a hundred skilled historians could ever catalog. But that is only the beginning. *A thousand years are like a day.* The span of human history is immense, covering roughly six thousand years so far. No historian can accurately synthesize the requisite details of human history into anything resembling gospel truth. But God can. He is not daunted by the scope of time, the immensity of eons and epochs and eras and dynasties. His processing ability is limitless. This is the subject matter of our heavenly history course: every single day of every person from every tribe and nation on earth, woven into a comprehensive and comprehendible narrative by the perfect Teacher.

Let me illustrate the idea of dimensions and details. Imagine you wanted to learn about the redwood forest in northern California. A friend of yours who works there happens to be a forestry expert specializing in the composition of redwood bark. But instead of zooming in on the bark of one tree, he wisely begins your education by hiring a friend who gives helicopter tours of Redwood National Park and the spectacular rocky cliffs that make up the Pacific shoreline. For two full days, you fly up and down the coastline, seeing over 110,000 acres of redwood trees and fifty miles of staggeringly beautiful California coastline from an altitude of one thousand feet. After that, your forestry friend gives you a daylong overview of the biology of individual redwoods, from root to crown. At last, after this three-day introduction, you are ready to study with him the bark of a single redwood tree using his magnifying glass. And the study will be far more interesting, because now you have the context, the "big picture." You have seen both the forest and the trees.

That is what our heavenly tour of six millennia of history will be like, only infinitely beyond that.

A Sense of the Vast Scope and Complexity of History

The "longest" book in my library is *The Wall Chart of World History: From Earliest Times to the Present* by Professor Edward Hull. Published in 1988, it seeks to cover human history from Adam and Eve to Ronald Reagan, Margaret Thatcher, and Deng Xiaoping. It is a unique volume, one long folded chart that can be pulled out panel after panel until it reaches fifteen feet, two inches in length. It is comprised of fourteen panels, covering 5,992 years of history (from 4004 BC to AD 1988). On these panels are multicolored "streams" (like rivers branching out) representing the various nation-states or empires that have emerged to dominate human civilization.

A single panel is devoted to the fourteenth through the seventeenth century, for example. On the far left of the panel (AD 1300) are twenty-five national streams. These individual streams are then broken into their respective heads of state, 382 in total. Only the names are listed, not a single word about them. At the top of this panel, a few significant events are briefly mentioned as well as inventions, battles, and leaders who were not heads of state. Despite all this detail, this panel does not even mention Japan, Mongolia, southeast Asia, Africa, South America, Central America, or North America.

This wall chart is an amazing achievement of scholarship and must have taken Professor Hull a long time to conceive, research, and accomplish. Yet despite its staggering level of complexity, it is childishly simple compared to the comprehensive dimensions and details that will flow into our resurrected eyes and minds when God begins to show us what he has done in every generation "for the praise of his glory."

God's Sovereign Reign over Human History Asserted in Scripture

It is God's reign over human history that will make the heavenly history lesson overpoweringly glorious. History is not "time + chance." History is a carefully wrought plan that God perfectly executes. We see this throughout Scripture.

1. God's throne rules infinitely above all nations. Isaiah said God sits enthroned above the earth, and the nations are as nothing before this throne: "Behold, the nations are like a drop from a bucket, and are accounted as the dust on the scales; behold, he takes up the coastlands like fine dust" (Isa. 40:15). It is effortless for God to rule over the rise and fall of mighty nations.

2. God sovereignly decides the boundaries of all nations. Some nations are mighty in size, population, power, and duration. Others are tiny, weak, and short-lived. This dynamic in every era of history powers the events of that time, and God actively rules over it. "[God] made from one man every nation of mankind to live on all the face of the earth, having determined allotted periods and the boundaries of their dwelling place" (Acts 17:26). In other words, God decides the duration of kingdoms and empires and what their boundaries should be. God has a redemptive purpose in this: "so that they might seek God, and perhaps they might reach

out and find him, though he is not far from each one of us"
(v. 27 CSB). Of course, this means that the conquests and
empire expansions of pagan rulers have been actively controlled by almighty God. When Incan prince Pachacuti (the
"Earth-shaker") defeated the neighboring Chanca people in
a battle in the Cuzco Valley of Peru (c. 1438), he began to
grow his little village in its secluded valley until it became
the capital of the vast Incan Empire. This empire lasted until
the Spanish conquistadors finally toppled it in 1572. The rise
and fall of the Incan Empire was ordained by God and part
of his sovereign plan. As was the rise of Genghis Khan from
1206 to 1227, and his victories that led to the Mongolian
Empire—the largest contiguous empire the world has ever
seen. God determined the boundaries in space and time of
every kingdom that has ever existed on Planet Earth, no
matter how small or great.

3. *God actively works to produce military conquests.*
Christians celebrate the direct activity of God in driving
out the Canaanite nations before the armies of Israel under
Joshua. But God has done the same thing for gentile nations
as well. Moses said God drove out the Zamzummites before
the Ammonites, the Horites before the Edomites, and the
Avvim before the Caphtorites (Deut. 2:20–23). All six of
these were gentile nations. God's sovereign plan is imple-
mented all over the globe, including among the Plains Indi-
ans in North America, such as the Sioux, Ojibwe, Navajo,
and Apache peoples, who were warring with each other and
building their own empires before the Europeans came and
conquered them.

4. *God has control over the minds of kings.* Essential to
God's sovereignty over history is his direct control over the

decisions of kings and emperors, the "movers and shakers" of every generation. While these leaders had freedom of thought and responsibility for their actions, Scripture asserts "The king's heart is a stream of water in the hand of the LORD; he turns it wherever he will" (Prov. 21:1). So a king's decision to turn to the left or right is in the hand of God. And the heavenly review of all those decisions will show how and why God used them to achieve his sovereign purposes.

5. *God rules over human outcomes.* Human purposes are all subject to the higher will of God. And when a mighty ruler determines to do something contrary to God's inscrutable purposes, God simply says no. We see this in the determination of some minor Palestinian kings to topple the Davidic king from the throne of Judah: "This is what the LORD God says: It will not happen; it will not occur" (Isa. 7:7 CSB). That settled the matter.

6. *God forcefully moves mighty tyrants.* God often likens mighty empires and their tyrannical rulers to beasts (Daniel 7; Revelation 13). God can control these beasts, maneuvering them wherever and whenever he chooses. As he said to Sennacherib, king of the mighty Assyrians: "I will put my hook in your nose and my bit in your mouth; I will make you go back the way you came" (Isa. 37:29 CSB). God is the ultimate animal trainer, controlling the mightiest beasts for his sovereign purposes.

7. *God has sovereign control over essential technologies.* Human science—ingenuity and invention—is essential to the rise and fall of nations, especially military conquests. The top-secret development of "Greek fire," which could not be extinguished by water but rather was spread by it, was essential to the Byzantine Empire's ability to resist the advance of

Islam for hundreds of years. But that great kingdom was conquered when the development of gunpowder and cannons led to the destruction of the walls of Constantinople in 1453. Later, the superior technology of European powers enabled them to conquer and colonize indigenous peoples in Africa, America, and Asia for over four centuries. Europeans were not genetically superior to those they conquered, but their technologies gave them a decisive edge. Thomas Edison said that genius is "one percent inspiration, ninety-nine percent perspiration."[2] But the "inspiration" that enables geniuses to devise new inventions comes ultimately from God. "God gave Solomon wisdom and understanding beyond measure, and breadth of mind like the sand on the seashore, so that Solomon's wisdom surpassed the wisdom of all the people of the east and all the wisdom of Egypt" (1 Kings 4:29–30). God's giving technological genius to certain peoples and withholding it from others has largely shaped the world. In heaven, God will reveal why he did what he did.

8. *God has control over commerce and trade.* The buying and selling of goods and the movement of money have contributed to the ebbs and flows of human history as well. God understands world economics better than the magnates of any era. The ancient empire of Tyre and its commercial power was much like Babylon and its military prowess. In Ezekiel 28, Satan is revealed as the mysterious "king of Tyre." But God rules over Satan, including commercial successes or failures. How and why God has opened his hand and given prosperity to some people—the dimensions and scope of their empires of trade—will be revealed in heaven: for example, the Arabic merchants of the Indian Ocean, the Hanseatic Union of northern Europe, the Medici, the Roth-

schilds, the Fuggers and the "robber barons," the Rockefell-
ers, as well as Jeff Bezos and his Amazon empire.

    9. God will bring his righteous judgment upon evil rulers.
Heaven will reveal how evil the hearts of human rulers were,
in most cases, but also how pure and holy God's purposes
always are. And God will make it clear how all the wicked
rulers of history were, in the end, brought to a perfect justice. Habakkuk 2 is an amazing overview of God's purposes
in history. First, "the righteous shall live by his faith" (v. 4).
Individual sinners will be justified (saved eternally) through
their faith in God. Second, God has decreed woe and judgment on the wicked of this world who build their empires
by crime and bloodshed. The cup of bloody conquest they
handed to their neighbors will eventually come around to
them, as the common phrase says: "What goes around comes
around." All the mighty buildings and impressive displays of
their empires will end up as fuel for the fire, and the arrogant
empire-builders will have labored for nothing (vv. 6–13).

    Third, God is building his own mighty empire that will
cover the world, and "the earth will be filled with the knowledge of the glory of the LORD as the waters cover the sea"
(v. 14). In the end, all the empires of humankind will be
consumed in the fires of judgment, but the empire of God
will shine with his glory for all eternity. Habakkuk 2 does not
specifically mention the Babylonians, or the Medo-Persians
that came next, or the Greeks that followed, or the Romans
that came after them . . . or the Visigoths or Vandals or Huns
or Vikings or Mongols or Ottomans or Spanish or French
or British or Germans or Americans or any of the great
empires that have trampled the earth as time has unfolded.
It just gives the general recipe: "Woe to him who builds an

empire by bloodshed." If the shoe fits, they will wear it . . . for all eternity.

Every specific example will be on display in the heavenly review. Sometimes divine judgment has been instantaneous, as when Herod was acclaimed to be a god and then immediately was struck down by an angel of the Lord, was eaten by worms, and died (Acts 12:23). Sometimes God has borne with the tyrant patiently for a long time and brought no obvious judgments in his or her lifetime, as with Mao Zedong, whose brutal twentieth-century reign in China resulted in the deaths of thirty to sixty million people, but who died peacefully in his bed at the age of eighty-two, at the height of his power. God's ways are truly not our ways, and not all his judgments appear obvious at the time. But the heavenly perspective will vindicate the wisdom, patience, power, and justice of God.

10. *God laughs over the futility of opposition.* Psalm 2:1–2 depicts the utter futility of all human efforts at stopping the spread of the kingdom of the Son of God. "The one enthroned in heaven laughs; the Lord ridicules them" (v. 4 CSB). The full history of those plots and conspiracies against the spread of the gospel of Jesus Christ will only be known in heaven, and when it is revealed, all of heaven will join in God's laughter over the puny efforts of humanity against Christ! The heavenly laughter will rise when we see how God actually used their plots to advance the gospel. The Roman Caesars plotted to stop the gospel by murdering Christians, but "the blood of martyrs was seed" for the even wider spread of Christianity. Voltaire mocked Christianity and the Bible, saying that within one generation no one would be reading the Bible except as a historical curiosity, but God orchestrated that the French

Bible society would use Voltaire's house as a Bible distribution center.[3] My missions professor, the late Christy Wilson, told how Chairman Mao and the Chinese Communist Party (CCP) sought to eradicate Christianity from China. To keep believers from having fellowship together, the CCP decided to scatter them all over the country. When Dr. Wilson told this story, he was laughing as he said, "The Chinese communists became the greatest mission sending agency of the twentieth century in China!" Furthermore, he said the Party leaders in the various locales wanted to humiliate Christians further, and so they gave them menial jobs like collecting garbage, for which they had to go house-to-house. What do you think those zealous Chinese Christians did as they went daily from one house to the next? Within one generation, the number of Chinese Christians exploded exponentially!

We will spend eternity celebrating the way our sovereign God wrote the sheet music for history before time began, and then played the "movers and shakers" like a virtuoso artist, hitting every note to perfection.

The Kingdom of Heaven Is Like Yeast

Jesus likened the kingdom of heaven to yeast hidden (*enkrupto*) in a large amount of flour that secretly permeated the whole batch of dough (Matt. 13:33). The advance of the kingdom of Christ began in one specific city, Jerusalem, at one specific time. Over the last twenty centuries, it has permeated the entire world, reaching geographically to the ends of the earth, infiltrating every single political nation, dominating world history incalculably. Every day of human history, the most significant things that are happening have to do with the advance of the kingdom of Christ from person to person. But that progress has been hidden, day after day. It is not tracked by mainstream media like the *New York Times*, CNN, Fox News, or the BBC.

Another parable teaches the same lesson:

> A man scatters seed on the ground. He sleeps and rises night and day; the seed sprouts and grows, although *he doesn't know how*. The soil produces a crop by itself—first the blade, then the head, and then the full grain on the head. As soon as the crop is ready, he sends for the sickle, because harvest has come. (Mark 4:26–29 CSB)

The kingdom of God advances in ways that people cannot understand. But in heaven, we will "know how." God's glory in the spread of the gospel to the ends of the earth will be fully unveiled in its dimensions and details. And the view will be staggering!

The Future Glory of the Heavenly Review

Even with all the work still to be done, it is wonderful to see in big-picture relief the journey that the church of Jesus Christ has traveled from one small room in Jerusalem to this present level of geographical extent and numerical splendor. In every generation, the Holy Spirit ensures that the name of Jesus Christ is the greatest name on earth, despite the fact that no infant is ever born into the world knowing anything about him at all. The Holy Spirit has orchestrated the protection of that name and of the truths of the gospel in every generation. He has worked across the centuries to defend the gospel and to move human messengers to spread it in their families and neighborhoods and, in the course of their trade and daily lives, to those of other places. He has defended the church of Jesus Christ from the false doctrines of Arianism, Pelagianism, semi-Pelagianism, and all other heresies.

He has secretly and mysteriously orchestrated the minds of mighty potentates to make rulings favorable to the spread of the gospel. He has controlled the economic conditions of nations to create the specific circumstances his sovereign will deemed best. He has maneuvered his messengers to cross forbidding mountain ranges and raging rivers to reach terrifying barbarian tribes in the dark forests beyond. He has raised up men and women to get on sailing vessels, travel as far as sixteen thousand nautical miles (in the case of John Paton from Scotland to the New Hebrides islands), and face likely death, such as at the hands of cannibals. He has moved missionaries to pack their belongings in their own coffins and travel to the west coast of Africa, expecting not to survive more than eighteen months in the unfamiliar disease–infested jungles. And most significantly, he has caused Christian parents all over the world to raise up the next generation in the nurture and admonition of the Lord, teaching their children the gospel of Jesus Christ in their native tongue.

The dimensions and details of the achievements of the triune God in this astonishing journey will not be scraped onto the trash heap of forgetfulness when the new universe comes. Rather, every redeemed child of God will receive an eternal heavenly education in what was done to bring them all there. And God will be greatly glorified in their resurrected hearts as he reveals new aspects of his glory in wave upon wave of heavenly review.

CHAPTER 7

Honoring Heroes,
Worshiping God

I recently fulfilled a dream of mine when I visited Westminster Abbey in London. It is the equivalent of Britain's national "Hall of Fame," as many of their greatest heroes are buried or honored there. My time was limited, and as awesome as the medieval architecture was, I was there primarily to gaze at the stone memorials that packed each side of the walkway. Most of the people honored there were unfamiliar to me, and I wrote down some of their names for future study. But I recognized some: Isaac Newton, the inventor of physics, calculus, and optics; George Frideric Handel, composer of *Messiah*; Geoffrey Chaucer, author of *The Canterbury Tales*. I made my way over to the renowned "Poet's Corner" and stood still, looking upward at the stone statue of William Shakespeare. His left index finger points to a scroll on which are written these words:

The Cloud capt Tow'rs,
The Gorgeous Palaces,
The Solemn Temples,
The Great Globe itself,
Yea all which it Inherit,
Shall Dissolve;
And like the baseless Fabrick of a Vision
Leave not a wreck behind.[1]

Fitting words for the overwhelming experience of looking at the best honors the living can give to the dead, these
crowded memorials in an old stone church. Shakespeare's
lines basically echo Ecclesiastes: "Vanity of vanities; all is
vanity" (1:2 KJV). Everything we see in this present age will
someday dissolve and be entirely forgotten.

Pressed for time, I had to walk by most of the memorials with barely a glance. When I stopped and studied the
tombs, I was struck by the brevity of life and the scarcity of
resources to properly honor heroes and their achievements.
Of the 3,300 people buried there, only 450 have memorials
in the abbey itself. The space is so limited, each memorial
seems to clamor for attention. And though a million people a
year pass through Westminster Abbey, the majority of Great
Britain's population will never go there or read the brief
stone inscriptions. This is the best humanity can do to honor
its heroes, and it is woefully inadequate.

For the heroic members of the family of God, heaven
holds the solution. The world honors its heroes in metal and
stone because the heroes themselves are dead, and those hard
materials best withstand the ravages of time. But in heaven,
such memorials will not be needed, for the heroes themselves

will be there, and the whole history of their glorious achievements will be perfectly revealed by almighty God.

Honoring Heroes, Worshiping God

One of the constant flaws of the sinful human condition is to make too much of human ability and too little of God's power. It may seem counterintuitive (even sinful) to imagine that any human would be the focus of adulation in heaven. When God sits on his throne before his people, allowing them to view his glory with unveiled faces, why would we for an instant turn away and gaze on a creature formed from the dust of the earth, or marshal our praise for a mere sinner redeemed from hell by the grace of God? Yet in heaven, God will honor all who served Christ (John 12:26). And if they receive honor from God, they will also receive honor from his saints. Paul told the Philippians to "honor people like [Epaphroditus], because he almost died for the work of Christ" (2:29–30 NIV). But this appropriate earthly honor will pale in comparison with the holy honor God will give to his servants in heaven.

God knows the difference between honor and worship, and so will we. They are related; both involve evaluation of something to which we are attracted or repulsed.[2] In worship, our souls evaluate the being and works of God as he has revealed them to us. In response, we give the highest place to God, the Creator, Redeemer, and Ruler of all things: "You shall worship the Lord your God, and him only shall you serve" (Matt. 4:10). We will not make the grave mistake made twice by the apostle John, who fell down to worship a glorious creature, the angel who delivered the visions that became the book of Revelation. The angel rebuked John then, saying "You must not do that! I am a fellow servant with you and your brothers the prophets, and with those who keep the words of this book. Worship God" (Rev. 22:9; see also 19:10).

When God reveals the mighty words and deeds of his people from redemptive history, we will not fall down and worship those men and women. We will realize that every honorable act they performed was through the prompting and power of God through the Holy Spirit (Isa. 26:12; John 3:21). The specially esteemed servants of God will know this as well. Privileged to sit on thrones in heaven, they will continually fall from their thrones and cast their crowns of honor before God's throne, giving him all the glory (Rev. 4:10).

Yet the honor they will bear in heaven will be great, and just, and right. For God will bestow it on them. And we will study the details of their robes and crowns and jewels so that we may honor them appropriately—but even more, so that we may learn more about God through their honorable lives and worship him all the more for the way they glorified him.

The Name above All Names

The word *name* refers to a reputation based on history. To "make a name for yourself" involves acting in such a way that people will know who you are and what you have done. The people of Babel wanted to build a tower to reach to heaven and thus "make a name for [themselves]" (Gen. 11:4). So in every generation, sinful people have sought worship in this pattern, that their names might be elevated and that they might attain godlike status.

Yet what so many have sought to seize by arrogance, God *gave* to David: "I will make for you a great name, like the name of the great ones of the earth" (2 Sam. 7:9). Consider those words! God determined to make David famous, giving him a name that would never perish. Part of our heavenly future will be learning the names of heroes and heroines that God delights to honor.

But the "name that is above every name" will be Jesus Christ. For no one served like him. No one gave up as much as he did. No one suffered as he did. No one lived so perfectly for the glory of God as he did. No one denied himself daily like he did: feeding, healing, teaching, and loving the broken sinners of the earth. And no one died under the wrath of God in perfect humility as he did:

> Who, though he was in the form of God, did not count equality with God a thing to be grasped, but emptied himself, by taking the form of a servant, being born in the likeness of men. And being found in human form, he humbled himself by becoming obedient to the point of death, even death on a cross. Therefore God has highly exalted him and bestowed on him *the name that is above every name*, so that at the name of Jesus every knee should bow, in heaven and on earth and under the earth, and every tongue confess that Jesus Christ is Lord, to the glory of God the Father. (Phil. 2:6–11)

If the Father bestows upon Jesus the "name that is above every name," it is clear there are other "names" in heaven— names of honor, based on deeds done in this present age. God will make those other names more famous than they are now. Yet this will exalt Jesus again and again. When some faithful sister in Christ is revealed as having denied herself to feed starving people, her sacrifice (however great) will still pale in comparison with what Jesus did on the cross. And she will say so with all her heart! And when some courageous missionary is revealed as having stood against the enemies of God and died for the souls of the unconverted elect, his sacrifice (however great) will still pale in comparison with what Jesus did on the cross. And he also will say so with all his heart! Hence every new revelation of the saints' glory will be another opportunity to worship the ever-increasingly glorious Jesus.

Neither Hagiography nor Graffiti on Monuments

In the summer of 2018, I was in Skopje, Macedonia, on a mission trip. I was taken on a tour of the downtown area and was surprised to find a remarkable number of statues—dozens and dozens of them—honoring great men and women of Macedonian history. These statues are a relatively new thing in Skopje, begun when the government commissioned 136 of them in 2010. The total number is now well over a hundred. Among those honored are playwrights, poets, governmental leaders, and of course, military heroes.

Every generation of people builds statues to honor its heroes. Some do it for themselves, like Saul and Absalom, who built monuments lest their names be forgotten in subsequent generations (1 Sam. 15:12; 2 Sam. 18:18). This hero worship is a sign of our fallen condition. Historians have often been guilty of hagiography in their accounts of great people. This involves an air-brushed depiction of a human life—selective recounting for the purpose of presenting a nearly perfect person. On the other side of the equation, hostility toward certain civic heroes because of later revelations of their sinful past has resulted in violence against their statues, from spray-painted graffiti to the bulldozer and crane.

But in heaven, there will be nothing but truth flowing from the mind of God as he reveals the past. Every saint began as a sinner. God's purpose in heaven will not be to shame any of his redeemed and glorified children. Rather our sins will be revealed only as necessary backstory to display his grace in both redeeming us and using us, flawed as we were. As Puritan leader Oliver Cromwell desired an honest portrait of himself, "warts and all," so we will be free from pride and concealment as to only desire the fullest revelation of God's atoning and enabling grace. The blood of Christ as atonement for the sins of the greatest and the least will be fully celebrated. And the power of the indwelling Holy Spirit both to inspire and empower action by flawed people will also receive its full celebration.

Some of the Heroes and Heroines We Will Honor in Heaven

For us to try to comprehend fully all the dimensions and details of the church's history is impossible. To borrow an image from Athanasius, it is like sitting on a cliff overlooking the ocean as it pounds the coastline as far as we can see.[3] From our lofty perch we can see a mile to the left and a mile to the right, and everywhere we look, wave upon wave of surf is rolling in and crashing with great plumes of spray on the beach below. We cannot begin to comprehend a single wave completely, and even if we did, there are countless more waves crashing farther up the coast that we have never even tried to study. And the ocean itself stretches far to the horizon, ready to supply an endless series of waves to overwhelm our mind and senses. So is the glory of God in redemptive history. Heaven alone will give proportional truth and limitless time and sufficient capability for the redeemed to study it. I would recommend we all read a well-written survey of church history to prepare for our future as glorified history experts.[4]

But to whet your appetite for God's story through the church, here are some of my heroes of church history, with some brief insights into what I think made them great. My purpose in this brief list is to give a slight foretaste of the heavenly revelation and the honor that will go on for all eternity.

Polycarp (69–155). In 155, Polycarp, the bishop of Smyrna, was arrested and tried before a Roman proconsul in the presence of an enraged mob for refusing to worship the gods. The climax came when the proconsul offered Polycarp freedom if he would simply swear by the emperor and curse Christ. Polycarp said, "For eighty-six years I have served him, and he has done me no evil. How could I curse my king, who saved me?"[5] Polycarp then courageously died by being burned at the stake.

Felicitas (c. 101–65). A courageous widow, Felicitas died for Christ during the persecution under the "enlightened" philosopher-emperor Marcus Aurelius in the year 165. She was a wealthy and godly Christian who spent her time doing works of charity for the poor in the city of Rome. Because she refused to worship the pagan gods, she was condemned. She boldly said, "While I live, I shall defeat you. And if you kill me, I shall defeat you all the more."[6]

Athanasius (c. 296–373). This bishop of Alexandria led the fight for the orthodox view of the incarnation of the Son of God "against the world." The majority of other bishops and government officials embraced Arianism—the concept that Jesus was God's first and greatest creation, not the eternal Son of God. On the night of February 8, 356, Athanasius gathered his loyal church for a worship and prayer service. The emperor's soldiers surrounded the church, then broke in the doors. Athanasius did not give way to fear but calmly took his seat on the bishop's throne and conducted the prayer service. Despite his people begging him to escape, Athanasius would not leave until all the people were safe. Then a band of loyal and courageous monks spirited him away. For the next six years, Athanasius completely disappeared from view, protected in the desert by loyal holy hermits. During those years of exile, Athanasius wrote some of his most influential works on the deity of Christ.[7]

Augustine of Hippo (354–430). Since the end of the apostolic era, no single figure has had more influence on the theology of the Christian church than Augustine. His conversion story honors the prayers of his godly mother, Monica, and is recorded in his *Confessions.* He was suffering the agonies of conversion, pulled in opposite directions by his sexual temptations and his yearning for Christ. While in the garden, he heard a little child singing, "Take and read! Take and read!" Intrigued by this strange song, he took it as a sign from God. He found in the garden a copy of Paul's Epistle to the Romans, and read the words that set him free from lust into the eternal worship of Christ:

> Let us walk properly as in the daytime, not in orgies and drunkenness, not in sexual immorality and sensuality, not in quarreling and jealousy. But put on the Lord Jesus Christ,

and make no provision for the flesh, to gratify its desires. (Rom. 13:13–14)

Augustine went on to write over five million words, the most influential theological works in the history of the church, setting the course of Catholic Christianity for over a thousand years.

Columba (521–97). Celtic monks set up a monastery on Iona, a remote windswept island off the coast of Scotland. Their leader was Columba, who established the pattern of the monastic order, focused on study, writing, praying, fasting, and bold evangelism. In 565, he sought to gain access to the leader of the fierce Picts in northern Scotland, King Bridei. Bridei refused to see him and locked the gates of his fortress against him. Columba and his monks began singing outside the gate. The pagan Druid priests tried to outshout them, but Columba had a more powerful voice. Then Columba began fasting and praying. Eventually (perhaps out of shame) Bridei opened the gates and let him in. Columba went on to lead Bridei and many of the Picts to faith in Christ.

Boniface (675–754). His given name was Wynfrith, and his most famous moment came in the year 723 at Geismar, near modern-day Fritzlar, when he boldly took an axe to an ancient oak tree sacred to the thunder-god Thor. The onlooking German pagans were enraged but waited for Thor to strike him dead as he began chopping. After just one stroke, suddenly a mighty wind came and finished the job, felling the tree in an instant. Boniface used the wood to build a chapel to Christ, and many of those who witnessed his bold act were converted by the gospel he preached.

John Wycliffe (c. 1330–84). Called "the Morningstar of the Reformation," Wycliffe was a dissident Catholic priest in Oxford, England, who rejected the authority of the pope, taught that all Christians should read the Bible for themselves, and boldly translated the Scriptures into the common tongue of the English people. He also trained and sent out itinerant lay preachers who were mocked as "Lollards" (mumblers) but who effectively preached the true gospel and won many to faith in Christ. Wycliffe died of a stroke before papal authorities could seize him, so his bones were exhumed and burned forty-four years after his death.

Jan Huss (1369–1415). Following in the steps of Wycliffe, Huss preached the gospel boldly in Bohemia (the modern Czech Republic) and sought to reform the Roman Catholic church in much the same way Luther would in Germany a hundred years later. He preached against the sale of indulgences and strongly emphasized the authority of the Scriptures over the pope. For these views he was declared a heretic and burned at the stake. As he was being led to his death, he declared, "What I preached with my lips, I now seal with my life." He died singing the Psalms.

Martin Luther (1483–1546). The German Reformer stood boldly on the Scriptures and risked his life for the gospel. His central doctrine was justification by faith alone, not from the works of the law. He translated the Bible into German, defeated Dutch humanist scholar Erasmus in a written debate on the freedom of the will, and shaped the direction of the Protestant Reformation. I believe that Luther would be the most entertaining of table companions in church history, with his sharp humor and quick wit, though glorification will cause all our brothers and sisters to serve as excellent dinner companions. To stand with Luther as he defended the gospel at the Diet of Worms would be among the most exciting moments in any visionary time travel the Holy Spirit might afford us. But just as moving for me would be to sit with him in his study at the Augustinian monastery in Erfurt as the truth of the gospel began to dawn on him.

William Tyndale (1494–1536). A linguistic genius perhaps unsurpassed in the history of the church, Tyndale made his life's work the translation of the Bible from its original languages into English. Early in his life, he openly declared this calling to a hostile priest who bore a tragically typical mark of medieval English clergy: a shocking ignorance of the Bible. Tyndale cried out against him, "If God spares my life, before many years pass I will make it possible for a boy behind his plow to know more of the Scripture than you do."[8] His brilliant work lives on in the King James Version, the most influential translation in the history of the English language. Tyndale's words account for as much as 84 percent of the KJV's New Testament and 75 percent of the Old Testament.[9] As he was being burned at the stake as a heretic, he cried out, "Lord, open the King of England's eyes!" Heaven will show the full effects of Tyndale's dying prayer, but within two years, the defiant Henry VIII ordered that the Bible of Miles Coverdale, based largely on Tyndale's work, be placed in all the churches of England.

John Calvin (1509–64). While Luther's central theme was justification by faith alone, Calvin's was the sovereignty of God over all of life. Calvin's great gift was his ability to systematize theology and to write with "lucid brevity."[10] His *Institutes of the Christian Religion* grew year by year from a brief pamphlet in 1536 to its final immense scope in 1559.

Calvin systematically preached through the Bible day after day, as well as publishing commentaries on forty-eight of the sixty-six books of the Bible. This combination of "the forest and the trees"—the big picture of systematic theology and the details of line after line of Scripture—gives a powerful methodology for drawing truth for every aspect of the Christian life from the Bible. The life context of Calvin's work was the Reformation of the church and the city of Geneva, in which Calvin established what Scottish Reformer John Knox called "the most perfect school of Christ that has existed since the days of the apostles."[11] If I had to choose one person in church history to debate against Voltaire or some other brilliant enemy of the gospel, I would choose Calvin.

John Owen (1616–83). The English Puritans were meticulous and thorough in how they lived, and their pastors and theologians followed suit in their writings. No one was more so than John Owen, a brilliant Oxford professor. He lived during the ascendancy of Puritanism in England and did his expansive work despite immense personal grief: he and his wife buried ten of their eleven children in infancy. I was first introduced to Owen's extremely careful thinking and writing when I read his *Death of Death in the Death of Christ*, a defense for definite atonement.[12] It was so satisfying to see how he addressed every possible text and argument in the matter, and he taught me to never set up straw men in any theological debate.

John Bunyan (1628–88). I can't wait to have table fellowship in heaven with the author of *Pilgrim's Progress*, the amazing allegory of the Christian life showing the perilous journey of salvation from the City of Destruction to the Celestial City. To see the creative process by which this repairer of pots, languishing in the Bedford jail, wrote words that millions would read all over the world will be to the praise of God's glory. But I also want to see the moment that three or four unnamed English housewives conversed on the glories of Christ, overheard but unseen by the unconverted Bunyan. He said "They spake as if joy did make them speak," and helped lead him to the Savior.[13] They are obscure heroines in the life of this famous hero.

Jonathan Edwards (1703–58). The most brilliant pastor-theologian in the history of American Christianity, Edwards tackled the difficult problems of divine sovereignty and human responsibility. He also preached the most famous sermon in American church history, "Sinners in the Hands of an Angry God." To see that sermon preached in Enfield, Connecticut, on July 8, 1741, and the secret working of the Holy Spirit causing unconverted sinners to cry out under conviction and cross over from death to life will be breathtaking, especially as we get to experience it in heaven with those very same people!

George Whitefield (1714–70). He was the greatest evangelistic preacher in church history. It is estimated that he preached over eighteen thousand times to over ten million hearers. He was hated by many of the unconverted clergy in England, who refused to allow him to preach in their pulpits. So in 1738, he went out to the fields and preached there to people who ordinarily would never have darkened the doorstep of a church, like the tough, irreligious coal miners of Kingswood in Bristol. As he unfolded the grave danger these unconverted sinners were in and the sweet pardon available through faith in Christ, abundant tears made tracks down their soot-covered faces. What will it be like to meet one of these converts in heaven, sit with him at the feast in the

New Jerusalem, and review that day as perfectly revealed by Christ? This bold preacher to millions also said, "God forbid that I should travel with anybody a quarter of an hour without speaking of Christ to them."[14] Perhaps we will meet in heaven some individuals who shared a carriage ride with Whitefield and whose lives were never the same again. On his grave he wanted this epitaph: "Here lies George Whitefield. What sort of man he was the Great Day will discover."[15] I think *eternity* will be long enough to discover all the details and impact he made on the millions who heard him and the generations that followed.

David Brainerd (1718–47). Brainerd was a weak, sickly, often discouraged man who fervently sought the face of the Lord in intimate prayer and meditation. He traveled into the wilderness for the salvation of the indigenous peoples of colonial America. His brutally honest journals, edited and published after his death at age twenty-nine by Jonathan Edwards, powerfully affected the future course of missions.[16] Missionary heroes such as William Carey, Henry Martyn, and Jim Elliot will sit at the table with Brainerd in heaven and say, "I read your journal, and it ignited in my heart a fiery zeal for the salvation of the lost."

William Wilberforce (1759–1833). Wilberforce was a Member of Parliament who led a brutal twenty-year campaign against the British slave trade, finally succeeding in 1807. He then took up the much more difficult task of the abolition of slavery itself. This did not occur until twenty-six years later, in 1833, with the bill passing a month after his death. The courage, perseverance, and moral clarity Wilberforce showed in this ambitious undertaking will shine in heaven for the praise of the glory of his Savior.

Adoniram (1788–1850) and Nancy (1789–1826) Judson.
For over two years, I read page after page of Courtney Anderson's *To the Golden Shore* to my kids, often moved to
tears by the descriptions of the trials and triumph of the
Judsons' mission to Burma.[17] It will be amazing to witness
Adoniram's time of extremity in a Burmese jail, hanging
upside down, tormented by ravenous mosquitoes, while his
faithful wife, Nancy, interceded every single day on his behalf
to the merciless officials. How marvelous it will be to sit at
the heavenly feast with the Judsons and the mighty army of
Burmese converts that multiplied over the generations that
followed!

George Müller (1805–98). He recorded over fifty thousand
specific answers to prayer, most of them on behalf of the
ten thousand orphans he and his mission cared for in his
lifetime. I have read of a specific day when he begged God
for breakfast for his orphans because the cupboard was bare,
and no sooner was the prayer done when a knock came on
the door. It was a local baker, who said that the Lord had
roused him in the middle of the night and impressed him
that Mr. Müller and his orphans needed bread, so he baked
it for them and was delivering it. Moments later, the milk-
man knocked and said his cart had broken down and the
milk would go bad if they didn't use it![18] So many lives were
affected by this Prussian man's steely commitment to "take
it to the Lord in prayer." Won't it be thrilling to go through
many of those fifty thousand answered prayers with the Lord
Jesus right there, explaining with delight what his purposes
were in each one?

John Paton (1824–1907). I don't think that anyone ever
traveled farther from home to arrive at his or her missionary

station than this Scottish missionary to the New Hebrides islands in the South Pacific (an estimated sixteen thousand miles by boat). His courage in going to reach a tribe of cannibals who had immediately killed and devoured the last missionaries who landed there is remarkable. Even more amazing is the secret protection worked by the sovereign God for this bold man, as time after time bloodthirsty natives bent on mayhem surrounded his home. Paton spent an unforgettable night in a tree communing with God while they searched for him with murderous intent. Heaven will reveal how God repeatedly dispatched invisible angelic warriors to protect him from the demons and their human servants before the gospel ultimately triumphed on those tropical islands.

Hudson Taylor (1832–1905). This pioneer of faith-based missions and trailblazer of efforts to get missionaries out of the port cities and into the inland regions, Taylor saw God do astonishing things in China. I want to walk with him in heavenly vision on the beach of anguished prayer, as he wrestled with the "accusing map" of the unreached provinces of China and their teeming millions. He surrendered to God's powerful leading to trust him for sufficient laborers and funds to reach them. I want to see all the answers to secret prayers, and also see how he learned the vital spiritual secret that "God's work done in God's way will never lack God's supply."[19] Imagine him looking you in the face in heaven, telling you about one of those times perhaps never recorded in any history book.

Charles Spurgeon (1834–92). Few preachers in church history have displayed the stunning level of giftedness of Spurgeon, who, like Chrysostom fifteen centuries before, was so eloquent he could have been called "golden mouth."

Spurgeon was a preaching phenomenon even as a teenager, and people flocked by the thousands to hear him unfold Scripture throughout his entire career. But it was especially as a soul-winning preacher that he was uniquely anointed by the Spirit of God. One day he was testing the acoustics in a new venue and said in his big voice, "Behold, the Lamb of God, who taketh away the sins of the world!" A hidden worker in the building heard him, thought it was the voice of God, and was converted.[20] Even printed copies of his sermons carried a similar anointing, as passengers on a ship who gathered around a public reading of a Spurgeon sermon caused a small revival to break out on board.[21]

Dwight L. Moody (1837–99). Moody was a simple shoe salesman who was called into the gospel ministry. He once said, "If this world is going to be reached, I am convinced that it must be done by men and women of average talent."[22] Early in his preaching ministry, he was devastated by the missed opportunity to preach the gospel of salvation to some hearers the night before the great Chicago fire in October 1871. Many of those hearers perished, and Moody never forgot. The zeal for souls remained in his heart the rest of his life, and he preached to an estimated one hundred million people over his lifetime. But like Whitefield before him, he was just as committed to personal evangelism. He resolved never to go to bed on any day without having shared the gospel with at least one person. Several times he retired for the night only to remember that pledge and go back out in search of someone to speak to about the gospel.[23]

J. Gresham Machen (1881–1937). Some are called to fight directly for souls; others are called to fight for the truth of the gospel so that souls may be saved. Machen was a warrior for the truth when theological liberalism was running rampant in the seminaries and pulpits of his day. For over a century, German higher criticism had brought one biblical truth after another into question, all while masquerading under the label of "Christianity." In 1923, Machen summed up the fight with his book titled *Christianity and Liberalism*. They are two different things. A denial of the truth of the incarnation, substitutionary death, and bodily resurrection of Jesus Christ is a denial of the gospel itself. Throughout the nineteenth and twentieth centuries, the battle against liberalism and "modernism" (seeking to accommodate science at the expense of biblical truth) was a central work of the Holy Spirit, who raised up many warriors to fight. Heaven will show how vital these warriors, including Machen, really were.

Brother Andrew (1928–). Born Andrew van der Bijl in the Netherlands, he was called to an astonishingly bold ministry during the Cold War, when communism was seeking to eradicate Christianity. Brother Andrew smuggled Bibles across borders and behind the Iron Curtain, earning the nickname "God's Smuggler." On one occasion, as he approached the border into Romania, he watched car after car being taken apart by the Romanian border guards, even down to searching the hubcaps. His car was packed with illegal Bibles. He prayed for the Lord's protection and felt led to place some of the Bibles on the seat next to him. As he came to the checkpoint, the guard looked at him and waved him on, not searching the car at all.[24] His ministry is one of many during that era of terror under many godless Communist regimes that we will study.

Jim (1927–56) and Elisabeth (1926–2015) Elliot. Jim is the most famous missionary martyr of the twentieth century, killed by a spear along with four other men as they sought to evangelize the Huaroni of Ecuador. His wife, Elisabeth, and the other widows lovingly and boldly lived among their husbands' killers and led them to Christ. Jim's most famous statement, written in his journal on October 28, 1949, has challenged me like few others: "He is no fool who gives what he cannot keep to gain what he cannot lose."[25] What immediately precedes that statement in his journal is wonderful for our purposes here: "One of the great blessings of heaven is the appreciation of heaven on earth." In heaven, we will study for all eternity what the Elliots gloriously gained for Christ. Elisabeth is the only one on this list of heroes whom I have personally met, as my family had the honor of eating dinner with her several years ago. The conversation was glorious, unforgettable, and a foretaste of the table fellowship we will enjoy with these heroes for all eternity.

Hebrews 11 Consummated

No doubt my list of heroes of church history will frustrate many of you. It frustrates me too! Some of you will ask why I did not include this person or that one, or this category of person or that one. All of us have our tendencies and biases. The apostle Paul chided the Corinthians for their factionalism, "I follow Paul, I follow Apollos, I follow Cephas." Paul wanted them to know that, in the family of God, *we get them all!* And in heaven, we don't have to choose, for time will not fail us.

The author of Hebrews undoubtedly felt frustrated too as he concludes his list of heroes in chapter 11, "*Time is too short* for me to tell about Gideon, Barak, Samson, Jephthah,

David, Samuel, and the prophets" (v. 32 CSB). He simply lists their names. He then lauds great acts of faith by anonymous heroes

> who by faith conquered kingdoms, administered justice, obtained promises, shut the mouths of lions, quenched the raging of fire, escaped the edge of the sword, gained strength in weakness, became mighty in battle, and put foreign armies to flight. Women received their dead, raised to life again. Other people were tortured, not accepting release, so that they might gain a better resurrection. Others experienced mockings and scourgings, as well as bonds and imprisonment. They were stoned, they were sawed in two, they died by the sword, they wandered about in sheepskins, in goatskins, destitute, afflicted, and mistreated. The world was not worthy of them. They wandered in deserts and on mountains, hiding in caves and holes in the ground. (vv. 33–38 CSB)

We will have eternity to look at each of the dimensions and details of the stories of each one of these great heroes. Mentioning their names now is like walking through an immense Smithsonian Institution of the faith, passing quickly by entire wings with names like "John Calvin" or "Elisabeth Elliot," and briefly switching on the lights and gazing down the corridor at a few of the exhibits. How much delight we will have in honoring each hero as the Lord lifts up one after another, saying, "Have you considered my servant Job?" "Have you considered my servant Esther?" "Have you considered my servant Raymond Lull?" And when we are done for a time honoring each one, they will join us in giving the ultimate worship to Christ, their King. For his glory they lived, served, and died.

CHAPTER 8

Obscure People and Events Finally Revealed

A t the west end of the nave in Westminster Abbey is the Tomb of the Unknown Warrior. It holds the mortal remains of a British soldier who fell in the maelstrom of a World War I battle and whose identity was lost. He was interred among kings with great honor on November 11, 1920, with an inscription that includes the words of 2 Timothy 2:19: "The Lord knoweth them that are his" (KJV). This memorial was the first of its kind in the world, and it caught on in many nations. In Arlington National Cemetery, the American memorial the Tomb of the Unknown Soldier reads "Known but to God." Part of the powerful impetus behind these memorials is the sense of injustice that could fill the hearts of soldiers willing to make the ultimate sacrifice of their lives for their country but who would then be completely forgotten by everyone in that country after they have died.

Forgetting past sacrifices is a central part of Eric Bogle's song "The Green Fields of France," written about the tragedy of World War I. The song is from the perspective of a traveler walking through a military cemetery. He rests by the graveside of a young man named Willie McBride. The second stanza speaks powerfully of being forgotten by those he once loved and ends with a question that twists the knife for us all: "Are you a stranger without even a name forever enshrined in an old photograph . . . faded to yellow in a brown leather frame?"[1] It is not only soldiers who dread being forgotten by those we leave behind. To think that all our effort and striving, laughter and loving, suffering and dying will become little more than dust in the wind is a concept many people find intolerable. Yet in this world, it is all but guaranteed. As the Scripture reminds us,

> As for man, his days are like grass,
>   he flourishes like a flower of the field;
> For the wind passes over it, and it is gone,
>   and its place knows it no more. (Ps. 103:15–16)

The very ground on which we walked, labored, plowed, planted, and poured out our blood, sweat, and tears will soon forget that we ever lived at all.

Obscure People Matter to God

Most of God's servants on earth have lived their entire lives in total obscurity. And therefore, their deeds of service that God used to build his worldwide empire are now forgotten. But we see in the Bible how much God delights in obscure people and unseen acts of valor. For example, the genealogies of 1 Chronicles list the names of many people about whom we know nothing else. There are 911 names recorded in the first nine chapters of 1 Chronicles. Over 90 percent of these names are not cross-referenced by my study Bible to any other Scripture. That means we know nothing about these people other than their names. Why did God want their names immortalized in eternal Scripture? One possible reason is that God wanted the millions of obscure people who would read the Bible to know that God cares about them. In his heavenly books, their names, words, and deeds are recorded and will be worth reviewing. Paul said that among us are not many wise, influential, or of noble birth. In every generation, God has specifically chosen the lowliest people in the world (1 Cor. 1:26–28). God cherishes the obscure.

Celebrating Eternally the Worth of Women

Of the nine hundred–plus names in 1 Chronicles 1–9, only twenty-five are women. In general, the Bible is written from a male point of view, and the words and deeds of men are the focus of much of the history recorded in it. There are, of course, noteworthy exceptions. A full and perfect revelation of the worth and value of godly women in the advancement of the kingdom of God will happen in heaven. To show the way God will esteem the hidden contributions of women, Jesus Christ spoke one day about the relative worth of a widow and her copper coins: "Truly, I say to you, this poor widow has put in more than all those who are contributing to the offering box. For they all contributed out of their abundance, but she out of her poverty has put in everything she had, all she had to live on" (Mark 12:43–44). This woman is the star witness in this chapter, for not only was she obscure, and not only was her contribution lost in the drama of the noisy giving going on around her, but she lived in a culture that ascribed little value to women. We must conclude that many of the most honored saints in glory will be people whose lives never made it into the pages of the history books. And many of the most honored saints in glory will be women.

Proverbs 31, for example, proclaims the timeless worth and value of a godly wife and mother. Her worth is "far more precious than jewels" (v. 10). Her hidden works of teaching infants how to think, speak, and act is the greatest pre-evangelism in the history of the church. And though I cannot prove it now, I believe heaven will show that the majority of the elect were effectively converted by their mothers very early in their lives. When they read the Bible all their lives, they read it in their "mother tongue." I think no other category of servant in the Lord's kingdom has had a greater hidden impact on the building of New Jerusalem than mothers. Proverbs ends with her honor: "Give her of the fruit of her hands, and let her works praise her in the gates" (v. 31). The "gates" represent the official place of business in the Old Testament cities. So, the perfect fulfillment of this verse is the public and eternal honor that will come to godly wives and mothers in New Jerusalem.

Hidden Heroes and Movements in Church History

There can be little doubt that stunning surprises await us in God's heavenly history lesson. Perhaps we will discover whole missionary movements, revivals, and expansions to new territories whose existence and/or details were never recorded in the history books. This dynamic began in the book of Acts, when the *non-apostles* were those who "were scattered [and] went about preaching the word" (Acts 8:4). These were lay leaders, of whom Philip was a prime example in his ministry to the Ethiopian eunuch. These are the hidden heroes who spread the gospel in their daily lives, using their trades and their travels to speak to whomever they met. As Jesus spoke of the hidden spread of the gospel like yeast permeating the dough, so the daily progress of the gospel has been produced by obscure servants of Christ doing things never recorded in history.

For example, what happened after the Ethiopian eunuch returned to his home in Ethiopia and resumed his official duties? Did he lead Candace, his queen, to faith in Christ? Any of the other officials? Any brothers or sisters? We will never know in this world. But recently, I came across a thrilling account of the early progress of the gospel in Africa. The author showed how ancient Christian literature and archaeology has proven the existence of a vast array of churches in Africa well before the year 180. Evidence even points to gospel fruit among the Punic-Berber people and other indigenous Africans. Yet the history books bear no record whatsoever of the missionaries who spread the gospel into Africa at such an early stage. It was "regular" people, perhaps merchants and soldiers living ordinary lives, who took the message of Christ crucified south into Africa.[2] Won't it be thrilling to see where all these African congregations came from?

Other great men and women of church history were somewhat famous in their day but have become obscure as time has passed. I have a book titled *Not Forgotten: Inspiring Missionary Pioneers* about the lives and service of eighteen missionaries, none of whose names were known to me before. One of them was John Lake, who founded a leper colony on an island forty miles from Macao in 1920. The lepers of South China at that time numbered in the millions and were among the most despised people in the country. Though Lake had been ministering to them for years, he'd had no base of operations. The island provided a perfect place—except for its infestation of pirates. Lake boldly shared the gospel with them, as well as his plan to build the leper colony. They listened to the gospel, and some of them also agreed to help build the colony. In the course of time, one of the most wicked pirates was converted and became a pastor to the lepers.[3] That story will be worth reviewing in heaven, as will the entire lives of those little-known missionary pioneers.

Consider Landrum and Sallie Holmes, missionaries in the Shandong Province of China in 1861, during the devastating Taiping Rebellion. After Landrum was murdered by a band of roving highway robbers, his courageous wife, Sallie, refused to leave China. Though filled with sorrow and loneliness as well as facing the dangers of being a widow in that era of Chinese history, she stayed in order to lead as many Chinese women to faith in Christ as she could. Along with another faithful colaborer, Martha Crawford, she went out from Tung Chau to the surrounding villages to share the gospel with Chinese women. Sallie was fearless. She knew that women were largely secluded in their homes and never mixed with men in public settings. Male missionaries could never gain access to them. It had to be done by women. Sallie and Martha would pack some food, pick a random direction, and set out on donkeys to share the gospel with women. When they stopped at homes, they knocked and entered, even if the woman's invitation was halfhearted or not given at all. Heaven alone will give the rest of us Christians a perfect sense of the final harvest of their labors.

The Southern Baptist Convention has sent out over twenty-five thousand missionaries in its 175-year history. By far the most famous has been Lottie Moon, another female missionary to the Shandong Province. Every year, the Lottie Moon Christmas Offering raises over 50 percent of the annual budget for SBC missions. Lottie learned her pattern of bold evangelism from her mentor, Sallie Holmes.[4] Imagine having fellowship in heaven with Sallie Holmes and some of the women she led to Christ!

Another hero of missions is James Gilmour (1843–91).[5] In 1870, Gilmour ventured forth into the vast Mongolian steppes from the city of Kalgan, northwest of modern-day Beijing. The temperature in the winters dropped to as low as forty degrees below zero. He ate small handfuls of millet and other simple local fare. When he lodged in Mongolian tents, they were covered with filth and vermin. He used some rudimentary medical knowledge (such as pulling rotting teeth) to gain access to various villages. He struggled with extreme loneliness and had a very small spiritual return on his investment. After four years of hard labor on the steppes, he could not count a single convert to Christianity, or even one person who had shown a passing interest in the faith. That he did not give up in despair is one of the great triumphs of his life. Later in his ministry, he did see a few people converted. During one eight-month campaign in Mongolia in 1886, he cared for 5,717 patients, preached the gospel to 23,755 people, traveled 1,860 miles, and saw only two Mongols profess faith in Christ.[6]

The account of the first convert Gilmour won, however, shows the infinite value of a single soul who comes to Christ. Gilmour was speaking with a Buddhist lama about the salvation of his soul when another Mongolian man came into the lama's mud-built hut. This man stirred the low smoldering fire in the center of the tent, causing smoke so dense Gilmour could not see him, even though he was just six feet away. But then the stranger spoke, saying "I have for months been a scholar of Jesus Christ, and whether this priest does or not, I am now ready to trust him." Because of the smoke, Gilmour was lying flat so he could breathe. But he said of that moment: "The place was beautiful to me as the gate of heaven, and the words of the confession of Christ from out the cloud of smoke were inspiring to me as if they had been spoken by an angel from out of a cloud of glory."[7] The next day, Gilmour walked twenty-three miles with this new convert, talking of Christian doctrine. In a lonely place in remote Mongolia, the two of them sat down and prayed together, then they separated. Gilmour never saw that man again in this world.[8]

James Gilmour was one of those heroes of whom Hebrews 11:38 says "the world was not worthy—wandering about in deserts and mountains, and in dens and caves of the earth." He often battled depression over the lack of evidence that his faithful ministry was having any eternal impact at all. His journals frequently recorded the words "Felt blue today."[9] We Christians love the stories of huge successes and well-known leaders of missions who have amazing totals of souls won to Christ. So a faithful laborer like James Gilmour, with his total of *three* recorded converts in Mongolia, can easily slip into total obscurity. Similarly, there are numberless other servants of the Lord whose labors were never even written down in this world. The true heritage of these forgotten warriors will only be fully revealed in heaven.

Hidden Missions to the Distant Islands?

It is possible that there have been whole mission movements never recorded in history. Heaven will reveal those hidden stories fully, for the praise of the glory of God.

In 1947, Norwegian ethnologist and adventurer Thor Heyerdahl proved his theory that the islands of the South Pacific, some of the remotest inhabited places on the face of the earth, were populated from the coastlands of South America by people journeying on simple wooden rafts that followed the currents in the Pacific Ocean. In the famous *Kon-Tiki* expedition, he traveled by a handmade log raft over 4,300 nautical miles from South America to the Tuamotu Islands in the South Pacific.[10] If he could do that by such primitive means, why couldn't God have delivered the gospel at any point in history anywhere on the planet by human messengers?[11] How thrilling it will be to get the heavenly review of all the dimensions and details of the spread of the gospel from Jerusalem to the ends of the earth!

Those Who Lie in Unvisited Tombs

The powerful movie *A Hidden Life* is about a farmer living a simple life with his wife and daughters near the Austrian Alps during World War II.[12] Franz Jägerstätter would have been completely obscure had he not been one of the rare men who opposed Adolf Hitler and the Nazis in Austria and Germany. He was a conscientious objector who refused to take the oath of personal allegiance to Hitler required of all soldiers of the Third Reich. For that act of rebellion, he was imprisoned, tortured, and executed. The movie's title comes from George Eliot's novel *Middlemarch*:

> For the growing good of the world is partly dependent on unhistoric acts; and that things are not so ill with you and me as they might have been is half owing to the number who lived faithfully a hidden life and rest in unvisited tombs.[13]

In every generation for two thousand years, the Holy Spirit has used "unhistoric acts" performed by millions of faithful Christians whose corpses were laid in a plot of earth with a simple marker that, within a short while, would never be visited again. They lived for the eternal good of those they served. Their honor will be eternal, based on the heavenly revelation of their deeds by the triune God.

CHAPTER 9

Spiritual Dimensions Unveiled

In July 1985, on the streets of Beverly, Massachusetts, the invisible barrier between the physical world and the spiritual was briefly torn open for me. I was doing street evangelism, and I noticed a very odd-looking man down one of the side streets. He was a street person, with shoulder-length hair and a long beard that was greasy and unkempt. Strangest of all, he held a long, twisted hardwood staff, which he was continually lifting and moving through the air in arcs while he was muttering to himself. As I shared the gospel with him, he looked at me with wild, unfocused eyes. He never said a word.

Several days later, I woke up in the third-floor room I was renting about a mile away. It was early in the morning, and the dawn was just beginning to illuminate the eastern sky. As I looked down toward the street, I quickly awakened more fully. There on the other side of the street, far below me, was this same wild man, standing with his back to the building I was in, swinging his staff in that same weird pattern! Why was he here? What was he doing? Suddenly he stopped moving his staff. Slowly he turned his head and looked back over his shoulder and up—*right at me!* Though I had not made a sound and was forty or fifty feet above him, across the street, he seemed to know I was looking at him. I couldn't breathe! Immediately I fell to my knees like I'd been stabbed. I began praying for God's protection. I continued praying for a long while until I felt enough courage to peek through the window. When I looked down to the street, he was gone. My skin was crawling at the eerie "coincidence" that this strange man had somehow located where I lived and was carrying out his odd ritual so near me. I never saw him again.

Beverly is only three miles from Salem, as in the "Salem witch trials" of colonial Massachusetts. Because of this reputation, actual witches come from all over the country to live there. The occult is openly practiced every single day in that dark town, and the invisible spiritual dimensions of evil seem more obvious in Salem. Whether or not this man was involved in the occult, I have no idea. In our Western materialist way, many would diagnose him with mental illness. But the Bible reminds us of the reality of demonic activity and demon possession. It also reveals that angels exist to minister continually to God's people. What we don't know while we live in this world is specifically how angels and demons interact with us on a daily basis. A glorious part of God's heavenly review will be a comprehensive unveiling of the activities of both angels and demons at every moment of history.

Our Present Perspective on the Heavenly Realms

Christians living in this present age are like the partially healed blind man with fuzzy vision, seeing people "like trees walking around" (Mark 8:24 NIV). This is especially true when it comes to the spiritual dimensions that surround us every day. These dimensions cannot be perceived with the five senses; they can only be recognized by God's servants when the veil is lifted by God's choice. When Jesus was baptized, the heavens were "torn open" (1:10) and the Holy Spirit descended on him like a dove. When Stephen was being martyred, he saw heaven "opened" and Jesus Christ standing at the right hand of the Father (Acts 7:56). And the apostle John, in exile on the island of Patmos, saw a door open in heaven and heard a voice, "Come up here, and I will show you what must take place after this" (Rev. 4:1). In the Old Testament, Elisha prayed for his servant's eyes to be opened to see the angelic army with chariots of fire surrounding them in the hills of Dothan (2 Kings 6:17).

Since these spiritual realms can usually only be perceived by faith based on Scripture, it is easy for them to recede in our minds. Westerners can easily operate in a "normal" way day by day, relying on our five senses and our scientific worldview, disregarding spirit beings like angels and demons as though they don't exist.[1] But many cultures are super-saturated with awareness of supernatural beings, to the extent that many people live in constant terror. In heaven, we will neither overestimate nor underestimate angels and demons but will be shown the truth of their daily impact on history.

From Mythology, Fiction, and Educated Guesses to Fact

The activities of angels and demons are well documented in Scripture. Sound exegesis coupled with seasoned observations can help us understand the actions of good and evil spiritual beings in daily life. But for the most part, we make educated guesses. Beyond this are the speculations of mythology and the work of fiction writers interpreting demonic and angelic activity. Martin Luther himself was steeped in the worldview of popular German culture.

> Certain elements even of old German paganism were blended with Christian mythology in the beliefs of these untutored folk. For them the woods and winds and water were peopled by elves, gnomes, fairies, mermen and mermaids, sprites and witches. . . . Luther's mother believed that they played such minor pranks as stealing eggs, milk, and butter; and Luther himself was never emancipated from such beliefs.[2]

Luther famously threw an inkwell at the devil while exiled in the gloomy attic of the old Wartburg Castle. He heard demons throwing nuts at the ceiling over his head and rolling casks down the stairs.[3] Beyond this, Luther believed that demonic forces were constantly assaulting his soul. But he had no absolute confirmation of the activities of these invisible beings, only educated guesses. How amazing it will be for all of God's people to look back on Luther's actual spiritual circumstances while he translated the Bible into German in that gloomy attic, to see the way God enabled him to triumph over demonic interference.

In 1521, when Luther made his journey to the Diet of Worms where he would be tried for heresy, he said, "I would go to Worms were there as many devils as tiles on the roof-tops."[4] This was more than just an expression for a man who daily felt Satanic fears, temptations, and accusations. Only in heaven, when we have the opportunity to replay Luther's courageous stand for gospel truth before the emperor at the Diet of Worms, will we be able to see what was really going on in the heavenly realms. Were there as many devils as there were tiles on the rooftops? And what of the night of April 17, 1521, which Luther spent in agonized prayer after his first day of trial at the Diet? That first day he had seemed timid, perhaps paralyzed at the display of his books and the demand to recant them all. Luther requested some time to pray, and it was granted. He was taken to his quarters, and heaven alone will display how both Satan and God acted upon this faithful man in those private hours. He wrote to a friend at that point, "If Christ is merciful, I shall not in all eternity recant a single particle."[5] After that night of prayer, Luther appeared before the emperor with astonishing bold-ness, unashamed of his doctrine.

> Unless I am convinced by Scripture and plain reason—I do not accept the authority of popes and councils, for they have contradicted each other—my conscience is captive to the Word of God. I cannot and I will not recant anything, for to go against conscience is neither right nor safe. Here I stand. I cannot do otherwise. God help me. Amen.[6]

This was a triumph of faith over fear. But only a heavenly review will tell us what demonic assault Luther endured and what angelic support he received that night before the trial and indeed at the trial itself. So it is with all great moments throughout history. When the heroes and heroines of the faith stood courageously against human opposition, we must conclude that angels and demons were invisibly active. God will pull back the veil to tell us "the rest of the story."

In addition to popular mythology, there is also the drama of fiction. The popular appeal of Frank Peretti's writings is directly connected to his vivid accounts of angelic and demonic activity. In 1986, Peretti published *This Present Darkness*, a novel in which angels are depicted in human terms, with national origins and ethnic features, carrying swords with which they do battle with demons. The demons are depicted as lurking in the inky black corners of the town and emerging like stealthy bats. This novel sold over 2.5 million copies worldwide and has powerfully affected the views of many. How much of Peretti's fiction will be vindicated and how much repudiated heaven alone will reveal.

God's Infinite Glory over the Heavenly Realms

In heaven, we will learn how infinitely great is the power of God over all his creatures. Christians are not dualists, believing that God and Satan (good and evil) are equal in power and authority. In our eternally glorious backward look, we will see that our Lord Jesus reigns on an exalted throne "*far above* all rule and authority and power and dominion, and above every name that is named, not only in this age but also in the one to come" (Eph. 1:21). How God created and sustained all angels and demons, and how even the most glorious angels veiled their sight in his presence (Isa. 6:2) will be on full display in our heavenly history lessons. We will see the truth of A. W. Tozer's words:

> God is as high above an archangel as above a caterpillar, for the gulf that separates the archangel from the caterpillar is but finite, while the gulf between God and the archangel is infinite.[7]

The infinite gap between God and all angels and demons will be obvious to us in heaven.

Reviewing the Magnitude of Our Invisible Enemies

The magnitude of God's spiritual enemies will be a great part of our heavenly celebration of his triumph over them. God allowed mighty monsters to arise, both demonic and human, and then wisely defeated them all. We will be able to handle that full display when we are glorified. I believe the main reason these spiritual realms of demonic activity are currently hidden from our eyes is that we would be paralyzed by a constant vision of their existence and power and would be reduced to quivering masses of immobile flesh. Jesus said to his disciples, "I still have many things to say to you, but you cannot bear them now" (John 16:12). God "knows our frame; he remembers that we are dust" (Ps. 103:14). Our "frames" are weak; we would be crushed under the sights and sounds of a full revelation of angels and demons.

Daniel's experience with the glorious angel of Daniel 10 gives us a sense of how impossible it would be for us mere humans to carry on ordinary life while seeing both the glorious angelic warriors that serve and defend us and the terrifying demonic opponents that would destroy us. The mere sight of this angel took Daniel's breath away and caused him to fall to the ground. Keep in mind, however, that this mighty angel was effectively defeated by one demon, thwarted for three weeks until God dispatched his archangel Michael to help him complete his mission to Daniel (Dan. 10:13). God seems to allow angels and demons to battle it out on roughly equal terms, though Satan and his angels are ultimately defeated and know their time is short (Rev. 12:7, 12).

If the mighty angel of Daniel 10 could not get by one demonic opponent (called the "prince of Persia"), how much more powerful would Satan be? The appearance of such terrifyingly powerful enemies would frighten even the most courageous servant of the Lord. God in his wisdom has chosen simply to instruct us in Scripture concerning angels and demons, give us some sense of what they are doing to affect the course of human events, and leave it at that. We cannot handle a fuller revelation while we remain in our mortal flesh. But when we get to heaven, we will be fully equipped to handle every truth God will lay upon us.

Satan, the Puppet Master of Empires, Revealed

One day the full drama of the rise and fall of world empires will be complete. And if the Lord wills to teach us all the aspects of Christ's mighty victory over Satan's evil domain, he will show us the full dimensions of that realm. Satan, the hidden master of the world, will be uncloaked at last. We will find out that the "conspiracy theorists" greatly *underestimated* the scale of the malicious cabal that ruled the world! Of course, they were thinking of "the illuminati" or the criminal underworld or some other secret human society with dark rituals dating back centuries. And some of that may well have taken place. But Scripture clearly reveals the existence of the true dark power that rules Planet Earth: "The whole world lies in the power of the evil one" (1 John 5:19). Though Satan does his evil works under the cloak of darkness, everything he and his demons ever did will be brought out into the open. We will see how every nation in human history was in some way controlled by a hidden puppet master.

In Isaiah 14, we see an oracle against "the king of Babylon" (v. 4). He is depicted as a cold-blooded tyrant who terrorized the world, beating down its people with unceasing fury and relentless persecution (v. 6). But then the oracle's language goes beyond what we would ascribe to a human king:

> How you are fallen from heaven,
>   O Day Star, son of Dawn!
> How you are cut down to the ground,
>   you who laid the nations low!
> You said in your heart,
>   "I will ascend to heaven;
> above the stars of God
>   I will set my throne on high;
> I will sit on the mount of assembly
>   in the far reaches of the north;
> I will ascend above the heights of the clouds;
>   I will make myself like the Most High."
> But you are brought down to Sheol,
>   to the far reaches of the pit. (vv. 12–15)

For centuries, many readers of this account have understood it to refer to the fall of Satan. They believe it describes his evil motive of pride, seeking to topple God from his heavenly throne, and is the backstory to the defeat of Satan described in Revelation 12, when the devil and his angels were thrown down to the surface of the earth. But if so, and I believe it is, why would the Holy Spirit call him the "king of Babylon"? I believe that the best way to understand this oracle is that God is judging *both* the puppet (the human king of Babylon) *and* the puppet master (Satan).[8] They both had the same overreaching ambition to build a great empire. They both sought to be worshiped, they both challenged God, and they both will finally be cast down to destruction. Since the garden of Eden, where Satan took over the body of a serpent to speak to Eve, he has been a master of disguises and deception. Paul said he "disguises himself as an angel of light" (2 Cor. 11:14). His true role as master of the world's human empires is hidden from our sight. We do not know which decisions and actions are inspired by Satan and which come from the evil corruptions of a ruler's own heart. The collaboration is biblically asserted but hard to prove in daily life.

Yet there are indications of Satan's control over the tyrants of this world. For example, Adolf Hitler had a deep love for the occult, controlling those around him with a volcanic temper that mirrored demon possession in the New Testament. Demons threw people down on the ground and caused them to foam at the mouth (Mark 9:20). Hitler behaved similarly, according to William L. Shirer, author of *The Rise and Fall of the Third Reich*:

[Hitler] seemed to be, as I noted in my diary that evening, on the verge of a nervous breakdown. "Teppichfresser!" ["carpet chewer"], muttered my German companion. . . . He explained that Hitler had been in such a maniacal mood over the Czechs the last few days [this was September 1938] that on more than one occasion he had lost control of himself completely, hurling himself to the floor and chewing the edge of the carpet. Hence the term.[9]

In heaven, the veil will be removed and we will be able to look back at all the rulers of the earth, great and small, and see how Satan and his demons manipulated them for their evil bidding. Even more gloriously, however, we will see God allowing Satan and the demons this freedom—and how they played into his purposes. The final version will be Satan's master puppet, the "Beast from the Sea" of Revelation 13, called the "Antichrist" by John, the "man of lawlessness" by Paul, and the "little horn" by Daniel.[10] That man will rule the whole world, and Christ will destroy him with the breath of his mouth and the radiance of his coming (2 Thess. 2:8).

How the sovereign God now rules over all the variants of this mysterious and hidden partnership—Satan and human tyrant—to build his own kingdom will be seen in heaven. We will worship God forever, amazed by his wisdom.

The Demonic Origin of All False Religions Exposed

Paul said, "What pagans sacrifice they offer to demons" (1 Cor. 10:20). This is a powerful insight into the supernatural nature and origin of all false world religions. Demons have been deity impersonators throughout human history, but we can only make this assertion based on insights given from Scripture. Our secular nation is one that celebrates religious diversity and toleration, extolling the equal virtues of all faiths. But true believers of Islam, Hinduism, Buddhism, animistic religions, and cults have long asserted the supernatural origin of their faith. The fanatical supporters of the cult of Artemis of Ephesus, for example, shouted that the goddess's image "fell from heaven" (Acts 19:35 CSB). Muslims believe that Muhammad had an encounter in a cave near Mecca with a supernatural being who assaulted him and commanded him to recite, resulting in the Koran. In the same way, Joseph Smith's supposed encounter with an angel he called Moroni in upstate New York resulted in his claim that he received gold plates from which he translated the book of Mormon. By this book, Satan has led millions astray.

Satan masquerades as an angel of light, and his servants disguise themselves as servants of righteousness (2 Cor. 11:14–15). Only in heaven will we be able to see how demonic all the false religions in the world were in both their origin and their daily exercise. As we look back on countless millions of Muslims who made pilgrimage to Mecca and bowed down in concentric circles around the Kaaba, we will see how powerfully Satan controlled that space and the hearts of the followers of Islam.

The dark centers of tribal religions in Africa and voodoo in Haiti manifest this control as well. I have felt the demonic power of voodoo practitioners during three mission trips to Haiti. The former slaves who founded that island regime in 1791 dedicated their nation to the tribal gods of their ancestors and drank blood sacrificed to those gods in a ceremony called *Bwa Kayiman*.[11] Many Haitian Christians believe that this "pact with the devil" explains a great deal of the two hundred years of suffering, natural disasters (hurricanes, earthquakes), corrupt government, and economic failure that have plagued the tiny Caribbean island. We cannot assert this with absolute certainty now. But heaven's revelation of the full scope of demonic activity in Haiti and God's purposes in judgment will be conclusive.

Ordinary Demonic Opposition Revealed

In heaven, we will be able to see the once-secret activities of Satan and his demons exposed. Their tireless and hate-filled efforts to stop Christ and his people will be uncovered. At the daily level, Christians will be able to see what demons did to hinder their prayers, their evangelistic efforts, their financial generosity, and all their good works. They will see demonic orchestration of tailor-made temptations of the sort described in C. S. Lewis's *Screwtape Letters*, where the experienced Screwtape trains a novice demon, Wormwood:

> You will say that these are very small sins; and doubtless, like all young tempters, you are anxious to be able to report spectacular wickedness. But do remember, the only thing that matters is the extent to which you separate the man from the Enemy [God]. It does not matter how small the sins are provided that their cumulative effect is to edge the man away from the Light and out into the Nothing. Murder is no better than cards if cards can do the trick. Indeed, the safest road to Hell is the gradual one—the gentle slope, soft underfoot, without sudden turnings, without milestones, without signposts.[12]

While we will see Satan's skills in temptation, the valor of Christians in putting sin to death will be revealed as well. We are left guessing that a bodily pain, or a distracting thought during prayer, or a cherished vase falling from the shelf may have been caused by a demon. As scientific materialists, we tend not to see demons behind *any* bush, while our brothers and sisters in sub-Saharan Africa or the jungles of Irian Jaya may see demons behind *every* bush. In heaven, we will have the opportunity to see it all clearly. We will see how God dispatched angels to protect us from demons; how he filtered specific temptations at particular moments of our lives when we were at our lowest (or highest) so that we would not be tempted beyond what we could bear (1 Cor. 10:13). Every single day of our lives, the devil and his demons assault our hearts and minds and seek to pull us from godly living. Seeing these stark realities would have horrified and paralyzed us in this world, but in the one to come, we will look in wonder at God's loving protection and give him the glory that our faith survived.

Two passages from *Pilgrim's Progress* can help us understand this heavenly backward look. In one of the most harrowing parts of his journey, Christian makes his way across the Valley of the Shadow of Death in the middle of the night. He hears terrifying and doleful sounds that deeply shake him. At the end of that dreadful night comes a welcome dawn, and with the light of the sun Christian is able to look back on the perilous way he had come.

> Now morning being come, he looked back, not out of desire to return, but to see, by the light of the day, what hazards he had gone through in the dark. So he saw more perfectly the ditch that was on the one hand, and the mire that was on the other; also how narrow the way was which led betwixt them both; also now he saw the hobgoblins, and satyrs, and dragons of the pit, but all afar off (for after break of day, they came not nigh); yet they were discovered to him, according

to that which is written, "He discovereth deep things out of darkness, and bringeth out to light the shadow of death."[13]

We will look back on our own walk through the "valley of the shadow of death" and see the "many dangers, toils, and snares" through which we came. And we will give glory to Christ for his sustaining presence and protection.

Earlier in the story, Christian comes to the home of a man named Interpreter, who teaches him key lessons about the Christian life with visual parables. In one of them, Christian sees a fire in a hearth against a wall, and a man is pouring water on it but cannot extinguish it. Interpreter says that the fire is the work of grace that God ignites in the heart, and the devil is constantly trying to quench it. But he never can! Interpreter shows Christian the back of the wall, where he sees another man secretly feeding oil to the bottom of the hearth. This man is Christ, who continually sustains the work of grace but in ways that the tempted are not able to see.[14] When we get to heaven, we will look back on all that Satan and his demons did to extinguish the work of God's grace from our hearts and how skillfully Christ blocked all those efforts.

The Secret Service of Angels Reviewed

God has dispatched angels to serve his children throughout history. Hebrews 1:14 says "Are [angels] not all ministering spirits sent out to serve those who are going to inherit salvation?" (CSB). It also says that some people have "entertained angels without knowing it" (13:2 NASB). Putting those two verses together, it is clear that angels have served the children of God in secret, hidden behind the veil that separates the physical world from the spiritual. In heaven that veil will be removed, and we will see how much they did for us. There will be no speculation or mythologies anymore, only the stories of God-honoring angelic missions.

And what were those deeds of angelic service? We don't know with absolute certainty what they do right now, or did in the past, or will do in the future. When Jacob had his dream of angels ascending and descending at Bethel, he was awed: "Surely the LORD is in this place, and *I did not know it*" (Gen. 28:16). So it is with the secret ministries and missions of angels. Every single day they are around us, actively serving, and we are not aware.

But Scripture does gives us basic ideas of the secret missions and works of angels. They

protect God's people from injury (Ps. 91:11–12)

fight God's spiritual enemies (demons) (Daniel 10)

fight earthly battles (Exod. 33:2)

kill people (Isa. 37:36; Acts 12:23)

deliver people from prison (Acts 12:7–11)

communicate messages from God (Luke 1:13)

communicate via dreams (Matt. 1:20; 2:13, 19–20)

maneuver evangelists together with lost people (Acts 8:26; 10:3–7)

strengthen the bodies of God's people (1 Kings 19:4–7; Luke 22:43)

It will truly be thrilling to see the innumerable ways angels filled out these categories (and many others) in service to God's people across all the centuries of redemptive history.

CHAPTER 10

Of Personal Interest

Our Spiritual Heritage

One Buddhist concept of heaven is nirvana, an eternal emptiness in which people lose all self-identity and become as a drop of water in an endless sea.[1] But we were created in the image of God as persons, and God will uphold that personal identity and awareness in the redeemed forever, minus the fleshly selfishness at sin's root. As a result, certain areas of intense personal interest will be ultimately revealed in heaven. Our unity with all Christians will also expand our interest to similar areas in their lives.

Personal Salvation

As God reveals the details of our lives on earth, the greatest theme will be how he saved us from our sins. John Murray's *Redemption Accomplished and Applied* divides our salvation into two main phases.[2] We know that our personal salvation was "accomplished" by Jesus Christ dying on the cross centuries before we were born. But Christ's blood had to be "applied" to our souls by the Holy Spirit in a unique set of circumstances. God orchestrated when and where we would be born, our family of birth, and the circumstances of our lives. He also determined when and how we would first hear the gospel of Christ, and how often and in what manner we would continue to hear it until we at last believed it. Looking back, we will marvel at how patient God was with us until we finally repented and trusted in him. We will see God's handiwork in arranging the right messengers at just the right time for us to cross over from death to life. It may have been a loving parent, skillful preacher, caring neighbor, zealous evangelist, or persistent college roommate (or maybe all of these in succession).

And once we called on the name of the Lord, God began his work in us, body, soul, and spirit, which continues every day for the rest of our lives. The Holy Spirit's power sanctifying us and sustaining our faith will be made manifest in heaven, for the praise of his glorious grace. We will be able to see how Christ continually interceded for us at the right hand of God (Heb. 7:25) that our faith might not fail (Luke 22:32) under the daily onslaught of the world, the flesh, and the devil, until we were safely out of this world, saved forever. We will give him glory again and again in heaven for this great work.

Personal Providence

Providence is God's sovereign ordering of earthly events for his own wise and glorious purposes. All the details of our lives on earth are wisely ordained and orchestrated by almighty God. In heaven, our perfected minds will be able to plumb the depths of this truth: "God causes all things to work together for good to those who love God, to those who are called according to His purpose" (Rom. 8:28 NASB). The $2.5 million "Grand Complication" wristwatch made by German watchmaker A. Lange and Söhne has 876 parts, each one handcrafted and hand assembled to form a perfectly harmonized piece of machinery.[3] Each one of the gears, sprockets, releases, springs, and jewels has a distinct purpose, though to the untrained eye that purpose is obscure. In the same way, God has assembled our lives and harmonized them with the lives of everyone with whom we interact. This is staggeringly complex. In heaven, we will understand the loving purposes of God in our early years, how we were raised, what level of poverty or affluence we experienced, how our parents interacted with us, the extent of our education, and our successes and failures along the way. We will understand the wisdom of God in the choice of our spouse and see how "what God has joined together" (Matt. 19:6 NASB) worked out in our joined lives. Puritan pastor John Flavel said it well: "It will doubtless be a part of our entertainment in heaven to view with transporting delight how the designs and methods were laid to bring us thither."[4] This heavenly "entertainment" will lead us to eternal worship.

Personal Harvest

Perhaps one of the most exciting revelations in heaven will be to see fully the eternal effects of our good works on earth.

We usually are not privy to the full effectiveness of our ministries. Perhaps God intends to keep us from becoming conceited (2 Cor. 12:7). This is the effect of the division of labor God willed in the work of the gospel. Paul said, "I planted, Apollos watered, but God gave the growth" (1 Cor. 3:6). Jesus said, "One sows and another reaps" (John 4:37). It will be thrilling to see the harvest of all the seeds of ministry we planted throughout our lives. I have shared the gospel on airplanes for years. Literally hundreds of people have sat next to me and have heard either some portion of the gospel message or all of it. I have almost no evidence that any of those seeds amounted to anything. Perhaps some were like the seeds sown along the path, that the birds ate right away (Matt. 13:4). But there may well be some people who will tell me in heaven that the conversation we had on a flight changed their lives forever.

Luke Short was a healthy hundred-year-old farmer in colonial New England who had not yet trusted Christ. Sitting in a field thinking about his long life, his mind went back to his boyhood years in Dartmouth, England, before he sailed for America. At the age of fifteen, he heard a sermon preached by John Flavel on the text "If any man love not the Lord Jesus Christ, let him be [accursed]" (1 Cor. 16:22 KJV). Flavel focused on the horror of dying under God's curse. Eighty-five years later, Luke Short remembered Flavel's sermon as he sat under a tree and came to faith in Christ![5] Flavel was long dead by that time. How many seeds do we plant in our lives and are never permitted in this world to see the harvest? Imagine the joy of finding how true it was that "[our] labor in the Lord [was] not in vain" (15:58 CSB).

All Our Prayers Finally Answered

We will also be able to see the full and eternal effects of our prayer lives. In prayer, we cast our bread upon the waters, and only in heaven will we find most of it again (Eccles. 11:1). Jesus told us that if we went into our room, closed the door, and prayed to our Father in secret, he would see what was done in secret and would reward us. Part of the reward will be to see the fruitfulness of prayers of which we were unaware in this world.

When I was in college, I received an Operation World prayer card for an unreached people group in Nepal. According to the card, they were the Bhotia tribe. I committed to pray daily for that people to come to faith in Christ, and for many years I was faithful to pray for their salvation. I even told God I was willing to go as a missionary to Nepal after graduation. On a rainy night, I knelt in prayer on Mt. Adams in New Hampshire. Alone on the mountain, I resolved to go to Nepal if God willed.

But God led me in a different direction. Over my years of praying daily for the Bhotia tribe, I heard nothing back. It was like shouting into a dark chasm and never hearing an echo. Did my prayers do anything at all? My wife, Christi, and I went to Japan as missionaries in 1993, and I stopped praying for the Bhotia tribe and focused my prayers on Japan.

Some years later, I went to a website listing unreached people groups and looked up the Bhotia tribe of Nepal. I was curious what had happened with them. I was shocked and embarrassed to find that, according to the website, there was *no such tribe* as the "Bhotia"! I did a little more research and came to the conclusion that it was true. It was as though

I had invested in a company for years that did not exist. My prayers were like letters sent by children "To Santa Claus, North Pole." I was so disappointed!

In the summer of 2011, my daughter, Jenny, and I had an opportunity to go to Nepal on a short-term mission trip, trekking in the Lower Mustang region of Nepal. I was excited to reconnect with the country that had long occupied my prayers, even if the actual tribe I prayed for did not exist. While we were there, we had the joy of working with a godly Christian named Shangbu. This thirty-four-year-old Nepali served as our guide and translator as we walked from village to village sharing the gospel. He was a strong Christian with a clear love for Jesus and for the people of Nepal.

As Shangbu and I were walking along the trail, I thought to ask him about the "Bhotia" tribe. I pushed it away, not wanting to experience my disappointment all over again. But the thought persisted. Nervously I asked him, "Shangbu, is there a tribe in Nepal called the Bhotia tribe?" I will never forget his answer: "Yes, that is *my* tribe! My last name is Bhote, and so the word is sometimes Bhotia or Bhote." He explained that it was the general designation for Nepali Tibetan Buddhists in that same region where we were trekking! We had been sharing the gospel with the Bhotia people all week! God had answered my commitment to go to Nepal someday and share with the Bhotia tribe! I also found out that Shangbu had come to faith in Christ in 1993, the same year I stopped praying for Nepal.

I felt both the Lord's encouragement and conviction. Encouragement: *Andy, I hear every prayer you pray, and I answer them according to my wisdom. Keep praying!* Conviction: *Why do you doubt prayer as much as you do?*

CHAPTER 11

Our Sins Redeemed and Painlessly Remembered

Whenever I talk with other Christians about a heavenly review, they eventually get a troubled look on their faces and ask, "Do you really think we will remember *everything*?" Most are troubled by the idea of going back over painful memories, things they would rather never relive or recount to anyone. Of all these, our sins are foremost. It seems impossible that we could enjoy heaven if we never escape memory of our worst, most shameful acts on earth. But I believe there is a way to comprehend heavenly memories of our sins without pain. And I believe that without memory of these things, it will be impossible to glorify God fully for the grace he has shown us in Christ.

Does God Remember Our Sins after He's Forgiven Them?

It seems that the Bible says the opposite, that our sins will be completely forgotten:

It is I who sweep away your transgressions
for My own sake
and *remember your sins no more*. (Isa. 43:25 HCSB)

Behold, the days are coming, declares the LORD, when I will
make a new covenant with the house of Israel and the house
of Judah. . . . For I will forgive their iniquity, and I will *remember their sin no more*. (Jer. 31:31, 34)

As far as the east is from the west,
    so far does he remove our transgressions from us.
        (Ps. 103:12)

You will cast all our sins
    into the depths of the sea. (Mic. 7:19)

These are some of the sweetest promises in the Bible, and
I do not want to undermine them. We will spend eternity
in a perfect relationship with God based on the atonement
of Christ. The moment we trust in Christ and are justified
by faith, we have perfect and eternal peace with God (Rom.
5:1). Christ's righteousness is imputed to us, so God considers us as righteous as Christ. God is perfectly reconciled
to us, and we to him (v. 10; 2 Cor. 5:18). That means our
relationship with God could not possibly be improved. He is
delighted with us and loves us as he loves his only begotten
Son (John 17:23).

But God has not forgotten our sins in an absolute sense.
If God truly does not remember the facts, dates, and circumstances of our sins, he would no longer be omniscient.
Since God is eternal, that means the past is as vivid to him
as the present and the future. Though we may forget the
wicked things we did as time passes, God experiences each

one as though it is occurring *right now*! How, then, should we understand these statements about God forgetting and removing our sins?

In order to understand the mystery of the infinite mind of God "remembering" and "forgetting," we must remind ourselves that God often uses anthropomorphisms when communicating with us. This is language that likens God to certain aspects of human experience. We read of various body parts of God, like the hand of the Lord, his eyes, his mouth, his breath, and so on. God walks in the garden of Eden (Gen. 3:8), sits on a throne (Ps. 29:10), and rises to shake the earth (Isa. 2:19). This language helps us understand God's actions in history.

In the account of the destruction of Sodom and Gomorrah, Lot's safety was in part ascribed to Abraham's intercession for him: "So . . . when God destroyed the cities of the plain, he *remembered* Abraham and brought Lot out of the catastrophe that overthrew the cities where Lot had lived" (Gen. 19:29 NIV). We should not think that God ever forgot Abraham and then suddenly remembered him, saying, "Oh, yes—Abraham asked me to rescue Lot! I'd better do something about that!" Rather, whenever the Bible says God "remembers" something (like his covenant or his promises), it means he is acting on the basis of that knowledge.

Therefore, when God says, "I will remember your sins no more," he is saying the opposite: "I will *not* act in accordance with what those sins truly deserve; I will *not* treat you accordingly!" Relationally, it will be as if those sins had never happened, *as though* God had no record, no memory of them at all. God's love and lavish affection toward us are as great as they would have been if we had never sinned at all. But that doesn't mean our sins never happened, for that would be a lie.

In the parable of the ten thousand talents, the king (representing God) cancels his servant's massive debt because the servant begged him to be patient with him. But when that servant found one of his fellow servants who owed him one hundred denarii, he choked him and demanded, "Pay me what you owe me!" When the king heard about it, he called the man back. "'You wicked servant! I forgave you *all that debt* because you pleaded with me. And should not you have had mercy on your fellow servant, as I had mercy on you?' And in anger his master delivered him to the jailers, until he should pay all his debt" (Matt. 18:32–34). The forgiveness of debt does not mean the king has no memory of the ten thousand talents. He remembers *the precise amount*. And so does God. God's gracious forgiveness means a perfect reconciliation, not divine amnesia.

Paul remembered what his life was like before his encounter with Christ on the road to Damascus: "Formerly I was a blasphemer, persecutor, and insolent opponent. . . . Christ Jesus came into the world to save sinners, of whom I am the foremost" (1 Tim. 1:13, 15). Paul wrote 1 Timothy under the inspiration of the Holy Spirit. The Spirit did not forget what Paul had done before he was converted, and Paul never forgot either. But still the grace and mercy of God flowed richly into Paul's heart through the blood of Christ.

A Painful Judgment Day

This fuller sense of the quantity and gravity of our sins will begin on judgment day. The Bible reveals very clearly that all

Christians will give an account of our lives to Christ: "For we must all appear before the judgment seat of Christ, so that each one may receive what is due for what he has done in the body, *whether good or evil*" (2 Cor. 5:10). Jesus said we will have to give an account on the day of judgment for "every careless word" we have spoken (Matt. 12:36). Paul fully believed that the doctrine of the resurrection from the dead meant that he should "take pains to have a clear conscience before God and man" (Acts 24:16 NIV). It did not seem that Paul expected to have an easy time on judgment day but rather that he should live every moment of every day in light of that meticulous accounting.

This inventory of all we have ever done while in the body—"whether good or evil"—is shocking to some Christians when they face the truth of it. We may squirm and try to evade it, saying "There is no condemnation for those in Christ Jesus." However, it is essential for us to realize there is an infinite difference between *giving an account* to Christ and *being condemned* to an eternity in hell for our sins. We will give an account; we will not be condemned for our sins.

Our testimony before the Lord on judgment day will be a mixture of pleasure and pain. The pleasure will come when we hear Christ's commendation: "Well done, good and faithful servant" (Matt. 25:21). The pain will come in having to explain to him our evil deeds—sins of commission and omission—especially considering his perfect love toward us. Remember when Peter denied the Lord, and Jesus turned and looked at Peter (Luke 22:60–61)? This face-to-face encounter with Christ and his sin was so painful that Peter wept bitterly. So will we weep on judgment day for our many failures. But then the Lord will wipe every tear from our eyes, and we will never weep again, nor will we feel any pain, shame, or regret (Rev. 21:4). We will have a perfect memory but no pain.

First Corinthians 3 points to a difficult judgment day for us:

> If anyone builds on the foundation with gold, silver, precious stones, wood, hay, straw—each one's work will become manifest, for the Day will disclose it, because it will be revealed by fire, and the fire will test what sort of work each one has done. If the work that anyone has built on the foundation survives, he will receive a reward. If anyone's work is burned up, he will *suffer loss*, though he himself will be saved, but only as through fire. (vv. 12–15)

All of our works will be tested by the fire of God's perfect standards. As we talked about earlier, the gold, silver, and costly stones are various good works that please Christ and will be rewarded. The wood, hay, and straw represent works without eternal merit—sins and worldly actions that did not build the kingdom of Christ. If what we have built burns up, we will suffer "loss." This loss is the missed opportunity to serve God and others, opportunities and resources squandered in things that proved to be worthless. Feeling this loss will be exquisitely painful, as will the process of looking Jesus in the eye and giving an account of everything we've ever said or done on earth. There will be tears of regret on that great judgment day, which the Lord will also wipe away, as we've seen (Rev. 21:4). Then we will spend eternity enjoying the rewards represented by the gold, silver, and costly stones.

Without Heavenly Memory of Sins, How Can We Celebrate Grace?

Central to our heavenly celebration will be the deep awareness of God's grace to us in Christ. In the coming ages, God will display the riches of this grace. At present, we lack an accurate estimation of how much grace God has lavished on us. We readily forget our sins, while we minimize God's perfect holiness. We do not know even a fraction of the times we sin in our thoughts, or when we commit sins of omission—walking right by needy people whom the Lord wanted us to help. When we get to heaven, our knowledge of our history of sin will be complete and perfect, so that we can fully glorify God for his grace.

The greater the knowledge we have of the magnitude of our sins—both their quantity and their seriousness—the greater value we will place on the atoning blood of Christ in heaven. Amos 5:12 says "I know how many are your transgressions and how great are your sins." For each of us individually, our sins are as many as they are mighty. There are a multitude of the redeemed, more than can be counted, from every nation on earth. How great must be the value of the blood of Christ to atone for such a volume of transgressions against a holy God! In order that Christ might have his due worship and thanks for such a great atonement, there must be a memory in heaven of the number and magnitude of the sins of the redeemed.

The Retelling of History Is Impossible If Sins Are Omitted

The tapestry of God's history is woven with the mixed deeds of all people, including the sins and good works of the elect.

How can even a single day of history be accurately recounted without an honest inclusion of our sins? The greatest sin in human history—the killing of the perfectly righteous Son of God—was carried out by men who may well be in heaven right now. A Roman centurion physically nailed Jesus to the cross, then watched in awe as the sky turned dark and the very ground shook beneath his feet. He heard Jesus's words of intercession, "Father, forgive them, for they do not know what they are doing" (Luke 23:34 NIV). The Great High Priest was praying for these Romans who were killing him in ignorance. The fruit of this prayer came immediately upon Jesus's death when the centurion said, "Truly this man was the Son of God" (Mark 15:39). If this centurion is indeed in heaven, when the death of our Savior is displayed for our worship, the centurion's actions will be shown as well. Imagine sitting at the feast in the New Jerusalem and talking with the man who drove the nails into the body of the Son of God!

So it is with all history, both sacred and secular. Human sinfulness is inextricable from its telling, and many of the key sins that have shaped history have been made by God's people, either before or after their conversions. To tell the history of the church without the sins of Christians would be like trying to read a letter from a soldier that was censored in World War II, with most of the words cut out or blackened by dark ink . . . not a single sentence intelligible. So would history be with all mention of our sins excised.

"It Is No Longer I Who Do It"

"If anyone is in Christ, he is a new creation. The old has passed away; behold, the new has come" (2 Cor. 5:17). This "new creation" language is used by the Bible to speak of the new heaven and new earth, where righteousness will dwell forever (2 Pet. 3:13). The sinner is "born again" (John 3:3, 6). The Holy Spirit removes the heart of stone and replaces it with a heart of flesh (Ezek. 36:26). The "old man" (Rom. 6:6 KJV) in Adam forever dies. Because of this decisive break, Paul can mysteriously say, "I no longer sin."

> So now *it is no longer I who do it, but sin that dwells within me.* For I know that nothing good dwells in me, that is, in my flesh. For I have the desire to do what is right, but not the ability to carry it out. For I do not do the good I want, but the evil I do not want is what I keep on doing. Now if I do what I do not want, *it is no longer I who do it, but sin that dwells within me.* (7:17–20)

The decisive break God makes between us and our sins at conversion is consummated in our actual lives at glorification. In heaven, we will be able to say with absolute truthfulness: "I no longer sin *at all.*" Paul cried out, "Wretched man that I am! Who will deliver me from this body of death?" (v. 24). But then Paul thanked God ahead of time for this deliverance through Jesus Christ in verse 25. And now it has happened; Paul is in heaven and will never sin again! And he is able to say now in heaven that it is not he who sinned but effectively another man, a man he will never be again. So it will be for all the redeemed. When our sins are revealed and reviewed as a necessary part of God's narration of history, we will have a *glorious detachment* from the people we were in our sins. Effectively the stinger of sin will have been totally and finally removed by our resurrection from the dead: "O death, where is your sting?" (1 Cor. 15:55). There will be not the slightest pang of shame when we watch our past actions in heaven.

No Scarlet Letters on Our White Robes

God will not shame his glorified people. There will be no "scarlet letters" embroidered on our radiant white robes. Public shame for sin is one of the most painful experiences that any human being could ever endure. Thomas Watson, in his treatise *The Doctrine of Repentance*, argues that shame is essential to true repentance.[1] God desires that sinners on earth would remember their sins, be ashamed, and never again open their mouths in arrogance against him (Ezek. 16:63). The prodigal son said that he was no longer worthy to be called his father's son. The tax collector in Jesus's parable beat his breast and would not even lift his eyes to heaven but said "Be merciful to me, a sinner" (Luke 18:13).

However, while shame is a necessary and beneficial part of the ongoing work of our sanctification, it has absolutely no place in heaven. Watson said, "If the sins of the godly are mentioned on Judgment Day, it will not be to shame them, but to magnify the riches of God's grace in pardoning them. . . . The saints will be without spot then and without shame."[2] Just as physical pain is necessary and helpful now on earth but will not be needed in heaven, so also the psychological pain of shame will become obsolete in heaven. As we discussed earlier, there will be no more death, mourning, crying, or pain in heaven. This includes the pain of shame for our sins.

According to the book of Revelation, the heavenly saints will be lavishly attired in white robes. The color white represents perfection and purity from all sin (3:4–5). Christ offers the white robes to the lukewarm sinners of Laodicea "so that you may be dressed and your shameful nakedness not be exposed" (v. 18 CSB). The redeemed from every tribe, language, people, and nation will all be wearing white robes, with no shame whatsoever (7:9). The apostle John was told that this multitude were those who "washed their robes and made them white in the blood of the Lamb" (v. 14). The armies of heaven that go with Jesus into the final battle are "arrayed in fine linen, white and pure" (19:14). Not one of those robes will bear an emblem of shame.

Yet robes will be needed in heaven. While the covering of our sins is perfect, the backstory is still there. Sin can never be spoken out of existence, not even by God, for God cannot lie. His answer was the atonement—the covering. The Hebrew word for "atonement" is also translated as "covering." Psalm 32:1 (quoted in Rom. 4:7) says that God covers our sins. God's holy eyes look continually on Christ's atoning blood and imputed righteousness when he sees the redeemed in heaven. But he knows our earthly careers in sin with perfect accuracy. He chooses to see Christ's imputed righteousness, the royal robe.

Walking around heaven, interacting with other redeemed sinners, we will see their glory, radiance, and honor—all gifts of God's grace. When we meet Paul, we will not meet him as "a blasphemer and a persecutor and a violent aggressor" (1 Tim. 1:13 NASB). He will shine as the trailblazing apostle to the gentiles who wrote the book of Romans. When we see King David, he will not be stamped "adulterer, murderer, deceiver." He will shine as a trophy of God's grace, a man after God's own heart, who courageously slew Goliath, reigned in righteousness, and walked in God's laws day after day.

Let the One Who Boasts Boast in the Lord

Throughout the Bible, God teaches a central lesson: it is not our abilities—our power, wisdom, goodness, military prowess, perseverance, loveliness, inventiveness, or any other attributes—that accomplish our salvation. God has worked in history to crush human boasting. For example, he commanded Gideon to dramatically reduce the size of the Israelite army that was going into battle against the Midianites, "lest Israel boast over me, saying, 'My own hand has saved me'" (Judg. 7:2).

God desires that sinners saved by grace would never forget their origins and would never boast except in the Lord: "For by grace you have been saved through faith. And this is not your own doing; it is the gift of God, not a result of works, *so that no one may boast*" (Eph. 2:8–9).

It is for these paired reasons—that we will never boast in ourselves again and that we will forever boast in God for our salvation—that God will cause us to remember our sins in heaven. The negative part of this—that we will not boast in ourselves ever again—is pictured as a silencing in response to shame over sin:

> Now we know that whatever the law says, it speaks to those who are subject to the law, so that *every mouth may be shut* and the whole world may become subject to God's judgment. (Rom. 3:19 CSB)

Behold, I am of small account; what shall I answer you? *I lay my hand on my mouth.* (Job 40:4)

God does not want us to become corrupted by our heavenly glory or wander from the glowing center of heavenly joy, God himself. Boasting in humanity rather than God both dishonors him and robs us of heavenly joy. The eternal remedy will be our memory of the sinners we were and how he saved us in Christ.

CHAPTER 12

Our Earthly Sufferings Fully Explained

The heavenly review of history will include God's explanation of the darkest threads in the tapestry of grace, the suffering of God's children. In 1828, missionary Adoniram Judson sat beside a grave he had dug in the jungle of Burma, staring into it for hours—for days. The grave contained no body; it was only symbolic. Two years before that, his beloved wife and partner in mission, Nancy, had died of a fever after a brief illness while Judson was away. That had been shockingly unexpected, for she had been in good health when he departed to translate for the British Army in their negotiations with the Burmese government. However, the health of their baby daughter, Maria, had been extremely fragile, like a flickering flame. While Judson was away, he received an envelope with an ominous black seal on it. Fearing the worst concerning his little girl, he tore it open and could barely believe the words as he read them: "Mrs. Judson is no more." Four months later, little Maria died as well.[1]

Over the next two years, Judson went into an emotional and spiritual tailspin. His glorious vision of leading the Burmese to faith in Christ and planting a church network was not even off the ground. Few had come to Christ, and those were persecuted by the increasingly hostile Buddhist government. A staggering investment had been repaid by a pitiful return. So, he went into the jungle and dug that symbolic grave. Deeply depressed, he felt at a great distance from God and his unfathomable purposes: "God is to me the Great Unknown. I believe in him, but I find him not."[2]

Why, O Lord?

God's servants like Judson have responded to the bitter twists and turns of providence with the anguished cry, "Why, O Lord?" David cried out,

> My God, my God, why have you forsaken me?
>> Why are you so far from saving me, from the
>>> words of my groaning?
> O my God, I cry by day, but *you do not answer*,
>> and by night, but I find no rest. (Ps. 22:1–2)

Job complained bitterly,

> God has cast me into the mire,
>> and I have become like dust and ashes.
> I cry to you for help and *you do not answer me*;
>> I stand, and you only look at me.

> You have turned cruel to me;
>> with the might of your hand you persecute me.
>>> (Job 30:19–21)

Like all suffering saints, Job cried out to God for relief and rescue from his circumstances and intense anguish. We want to be delivered from oppression, healed from sickness, and witness the unconverted saved. But if those things do not happen and our circumstances only get worse, we would like some explanation from God. "Why, O Lord? Why is this happening to me? What possible good can come from this sorrow and pain?"

These questions become more acute if we have a robust doctrine of God's providence, believing in his active sovereignty over the smallest details of everyday life. A sparrow cannot die apart from God's will, and even the hairs of our head are numbered (Matt. 10:29–30). God can convert any sinner, at any time—even one breathing out murderous threats against his disciples (Acts 9). God can effortlessly heal every sickness known to humankind (Ps. 103:3). God can make any prison door swing open, setting the captives free (Acts 16:26). God's blessing of his Word can produce mass conversions (2:41). Indeed, God actively holds together every atom in the universe, and nothing can happen apart from his will. Knowing the dimensions of providence both comforts and challenges us. We are comforted when we look to the future, for it is in his hands. But we are challenged by human suffering. Whenever anything happens that brings his children pain, we ask "Why, O Lord?!" And we find (along with Job and the psalmists) that God does not give direct explanations now. But I believe he will reveal everything in the world to come.

Some of you may feel ambivalent about that. It is not only our sins that we would like to forget forever and not carry into eternity. What about the most painful moments of our lives? Why would we want to relive the agonies of burying a child, the relentless pain of a long battle with cancer, the disappointments of ministry failures, or the sorrows of financial ruin? In this life, God mercifully gives his children a therapeutic amnesia, so our first experience of tragedy fades and we can go on with our lives ("Time heals all wounds"). But we will have perfect memories in heaven. What good can come from reliving life's bitterest moments?

Why God Will Review Our Suffering

God's darkest providences can cause serious doubt in his people, particularly regarding his power, his wisdom, or his love for us. Human suffering is the crucible of theology, and false doctrine has flowed from its hottest flames. *Theodicy* is the term referring to the vindication of God's actions in relationship to evil, especially human suffering. Christians who defend the faith in this groaning world must be able to answer those who question the existence of God because of seemingly pointless suffering. But no vindication of God will ever be complete in this world, because God's actions are often mysterious. The only perfect theodicy will be done by God himself in heaven, explaining the details of his beloved children's suffering. As the psalmist said to God, "You yourself have recorded my wanderings. Put my tears in your bottle. Are they not in your book?" (Ps. 56:8 CSB). God wants us to understand the necessity of each dark thread of providence to make the intricately beautiful tapestry we will review in heaven. His power, wisdom, and love will be perfectly vindicated.

Scriptural Support

God intends to reveal himself completely—his thoughts, purposes, and works—to his chosen people. God's self-disclosure began here in this world but will be completed in heaven. Jesus said to the Father, "This is eternal life, that they know you, the only true God, and Jesus Christ whom you have sent" (John 17:3). In Jesus's ministry, he taught in parables. Outsiders were excluded; insiders received detailed interpretations: "'To you has been given the secret of the kingdom of God, but for those outside everything is in parables.' . . . Privately to his own disciples he explained everything" (Mark 4:11, 34).

The Holy Spirit is in this present world to guide God's people into all truth (John 16:13). This full sharing of truth, nothing held back, characterizes the Trinity; Jesus said, "All that the Father has is mine" (v. 15). The Spirit's role is to bring the children of God into that possession. This process is not completed on earth, since we cannot now bear everything that Christ could say to us (v. 12). Our spirits are weak, and we could not handle full disclosure. But in heaven, when the danger is past, we will be ready for everything Christ wants to reveal to us: "I do not call you servants anymore, because a servant doesn't know what his master is doing. I have called you friends, because I have made known to you everything I have heard from my Father" (15:15 CSB). Because we are his friends, Christ does not want to hold anything back from us ultimately. Part of the love relationship he is working between us, himself, and the Father is one of full disclosure, not concealment. He will hold nothing back but will reveal everything to us as the consummation of his love for us. Jesus equates love with his self-disclosure: "He who loves me will be loved by my Father, and I will love him and manifest myself to him" (14:21). In heaven, this manifestation of Christ to us will be completed.

Consider God's internal question concerning his imminent destruction of Sodom and Gomorrah: "Shall I hide from Abraham what I am about to do, seeing that Abraham shall surely become a great and mighty nation, and all the nations of the earth shall be blessed in him? For I have chosen him" (Gen. 18:17–19). The Hebrew verb translated "hide" means "to cover up." Abraham was chosen by the Lord for his role as the "father" of the elect and was privileged to know the very mind of God. And five hundred years later, as Moses was writing this account in Genesis, the Holy Spirit invited Moses into God's self-deliberation concerning Sodom and Abraham! God brings his chosen people into the secret counsels of his will. Therefore, in heaven, God will fully disclose the purposes of his heart in his people's suffering while they were on earth.

Several times in the book of Revelation, John is invited into discussion about the meaning of the visions as they unfold. "Come up here, and I will show you what must take place after this" (4:1); "Come, I will show you the judgment of the great prostitute who is seated on many waters" (17:1); "Come, I will show you the Bride, the wife of the Lamb" (21:9); "I will tell you the mystery of the woman, and of the beast with seven heads and ten horns that carries her" (17:7). John represents all the elect in both their present earthly limitations and their future glory. Presently, there are some things we cannot know. John is restricted from writing what the seven thunders said in Revelation 10:4; it is sealed for the future. But other times, John is forcefully commanded to write down what he sees and hears because these things are meant to be understood immediately by the people of God (21:5). There will be a sweet consummation in heaven when God will hold nothing back from any of his children.

Many Painful Providences

Death is the "last enemy" (1 Cor. 15:26), and Jesus wept right before raising Lazarus from the dead because he knew how many tears his people would shed before his bitterest foe would finally be vanquished.

The death of loved ones, especially children. There is no trial more agonizing than the death of a child. Martin Luther was in deep agony over the loss of his precious daughter Magdalena on September 20, 1542. He wrote to a friend,

> My wife and I . . . cannot think of it without sobs and groans which tear the heart apart. The memory of her face, her words, her expressions in life and death—everything about our most obedient and loving daughter lingers in our hearts so that even the death of Christ (and what are all deaths compared to his?) is almost powerless to lift our minds above our loss. So would you give thanks to God in our stead? For hasn't he honored us greatly in glorifying our child?[3]

After the little coffin had been lowered down into the cold earth, watered by the anguished tears of the parents, many laid their weary heads on their pillows that night with one burning unanswered question: "Why, O Lord?" God's reasons will be explained fully in heaven, and no parents will grieve then.

Untimely deaths of fruitful people. When particularly effective and gifted servants of the Lord die "before [their] time" (Eccles. 7:17), those who are left to carry on the work wonder why the Lord took them so soon. How can we understand the early deaths of Perpetua (22), King Edward VI of England (15), David Brainerd (29), Robert Murray Mc-Cheyne (29), William Borden (25), Jim Elliot (28), and countless others? Read accounts of their lives, and you may find yourself growing in perplexity. Borden was a wealthy heir who gave it all up to become a missionary to China's Muslims. He died of spinal meningitis while traveling to the mission field. In our limited perspective, we think a long career of service to the Lord would have been far more effective in furthering God's kingdom. But God disagreed.

Accidents. Church history is filled with tragic accidents that beg for explanation. In 1873, the ship *Ville du Havre* collided with another ship in the middle of the Atlantic Ocean, broke in two, and sank within twelve minutes. Aboard were Anna Spafford and her four young daughters. Anna was rescued, but all four of her daughters died. She wired her husband, Horatio, "Saved alone." Anna said, "God gave me four daughters. Now they have been taken from me. *Someday, I will understand why.*"[4] As her husband was sailing to reunite with her, he passed over the watery grave of their daughters. He began writing the words to the hymn "It Is Well with My Soul" there.

Two of the greatest preachers ever, Jonathan Edwards and Charles Spurgeon, had similar accidents with very different outcomes. During a midweek service in 1737, the gallery in the church building where Edwards was preaching collapsed, but there were no deaths, nor even any serious injuries. Edwards marveled over this amazing display of the providence of God: "None can give an account, or conceive, by what means people's lives and limbs should be thus preserved, when so great a multitude were thus eminently exposed."[5] Spurgeon did not experience the providence of God so sweetly. On the evening of October 19, 1856, Spurgeon was about to preach to over twelve thousand people in the Surrey Garden Music Hall. Someone yelled "Fire!" In the ensuing panic, the frenzied movement of the crowd caused a balcony to collapse, leaving seven dead and twenty-eight seriously injured. The incident shook Spurgeon so deeply that he felt he would never preach again.[6] "Accidents" may seem random, but all are under the watchful eye of a sovereign God who could have prevented each and every one of them or delivered people from them. God owes no explanations, but in heaven he will give them.

Natural disasters (earthquakes, hurricanes, tornadoes, landslides, wildfires). God's involvement in such disasters has long been a source of theological extremes. Some deny that God would ever do anything that would destroy human life; others interpret natural disasters as God's punishment for human sins. For example, when Hurricane Katrina devastated New Orleans and much of the Gulf Coast on August 29, 2005, one TV preacher proclaimed that Katrina was God's judgment on New Orleans's sinful culture as well as a warning for the entire nation.[7] Other Christian leaders said such statements dishonored the character of God and missed opportunities to show compassion for the victims.

In heaven we will hear the official explanation from God about his intentions in every natural disaster that has ever occurred. And his explanations will be deep and complex. When a tornado sweeps through a town, it completely destroys some houses, damages others, and entirely spares still others. The homes of Christians and non-Christians alike are found in all three categories. God was doing specific things in each life affected, but his "paths [are] beyond tracing out" (Rom. 11:33 NIV).

One dies, another lives. Tragic deaths occur in which we can ask why one was saved and another not. Both John Bunyan and John Newton saw another man take their place at a key moment, leading immediately to that man's death. Another soldier took Bunyan's place on sentry duty during the English Civil War and was shot by the enemy.[8] Another sailor took Newton's place on watch during a storm and was swept overboard by a rogue wave.[9] Neither Bunyan nor Newton was converted at the time. Both felt that God gave another person's life for their own final salvation. Because Bunyan and Newton became great Christians, we can easily vindicate God's wisdom in these instances. But what about the opposite? There are many moments when God's rationale for those who survived and those who perished is absolutely unclear.

The sparing of tyrants. Why do wicked oppressors survive, only to continue their works of tyranny? On July 20, 1944, a powerful bomb exploded in Adolf Hitler's staff meeting. It killed three people, but a heavy oak table effectively shielded Hitler from the deadly blast. World War II continued in Europe for another ten months, dooming countless people (including many Christians) to death. On April 4, 1945, Hitler took one of the last actions of his tyrannical reign, condemning theologian Dietrich Bonhoeffer to death because of his involvement in the assassination plot. The lives of Bonhoeffer and many in the concentration camps, as well as in all the armies, were radically affected by Hitler's survival.

Corrie ten Boom and her sister Betsie were arrested in Holland on February 28, 1944, for harboring Jewish people in their "hiding place." They were eventually imprisoned in the notorious Ravensbruck concentration camp, where Betsie died on December 16, 1944. On her deathbed, she said to Corrie, "There is no pit so deep that God's love is not deeper still."[10] If Hitler had died in that blast, the Ten Booms' history might have been radically different. One day we will know the deep reasons for such choices in his providential plan.

Outbreaks, epidemics, and pandemics. Disease has played a crucial role in the shaping of human history. I am writing this chapter during the worldwide pandemic of the COVID-19 coronavirus. The effect on the world economy and society is incalculable. This virus is structurally very similar to the SARS virus of 2003, which infected 8,098 people and killed 773.[11] As of December 2020, the COVID-19 virus had infected 68 million people worldwide, with over 1.5 million deaths.[12] Why the one coronavirus should have such a minimal impact and the other such a massive one is a mystery. But disease and immunity have deeply shaped human history. Jared Diamond made this argument in *Guns, Germs, and Steel*, based on the impact of European carriers of diseases for which indigenous peoples had no immunity: "Smallpox, measles, influenza, typhus, bubonic plague, and other infectious diseases endemic in Europe played a decisive role in European conquests."[13]

What appears random on earth will be explained in clear detail by the Author of history in heaven.

The "Insanity" of God

In 2013, Nik Ripken published a powerful book cataloging his fifteen-year journey studying the experiences of persecuted Christians around the world. The book's title concerned some Christians because it sounded irreverent or even blasphemous: *The Insanity of God.*[14] Ripken's own questions began in Somalia, where Muslim warlords were systematically crushing the church while roving bands of young men were shooting innocent people in the streets. He asked, "Can the gospel really flourish in the hardest places on earth?" Around that time, his own son died of an asthma attack on Easter Sunday morning in Nairobi, Kenya, an attack he would have likely survived if they were in America. That church asked Ripkin a bitter question: "How can God allow your son to die on Easter?"[15]

These experiences propelled Ripken on his journey to understand the inscrutable purposes of God in the world's dark places. The so-called insanity came from the examples of mindless depravity of the regional warlords, who were allowing starving Somali children to sit waiting outside a compound that had just been captured. These desperate children, near death, waited for some scraps to fall from the warlords' table. Ripkin watched the children descend upon an animal carcass that was heaved over the wall. Like locusts, they devoured whatever was left so that they could live in that hellhole another day. A compassionate and anguished Christian asked the questions that burned inside them: "God, where are you? Do you know what is happening in this place? What kind of God would allow this to happen?"[16]

The provocative, controversial title of Ripken's book is based on this one theme: How can a loving, wise God put his beloved children through such overwhelming sorrow, pain, suffering, and death at the hands of irrational servants of Satan? There seems to be no answer to the details of that suffering. It all seems so . . . *insane.* Yet heaven will reveal that, while human sin is utterly irrational to the core, God is perfect and purely reasonable; he says "Come now, let us reason together" (Isa. 1:18). When Paul was accused of insanity by the Roman governor Festus, he answered, "I am not out of my mind, most excellent Festus, but I am speaking true and reasonable words" (Acts 26:25). The gospel is exquisitely reasonable because it comes from the mind of God. God doesn't do luck. God doesn't do random. God doesn't shrug and say, "I don't know why I did that." And God certainly doesn't do insane. God is pure reason as well as pure love. There is a perfectly developed thought process behind every moment of redemptive history.

Not only will there be a full telling of all of God's reasons but the explanations will be deep and rich, fully satisfying to the redeemed in heaven. Like a chess expert has delight in re-playing all the moves of a masterpiece game by Bobby Fischer; like a lover of music has delight in understanding Bach's use of dissonance in the final movement of *St. Matthew Passion* or a certain chord progression in his ethereal fugues; like a lover of football theory has delight in studying the West Coast Offense devised by the genius Bill Walsh; like a lover of science has delight in the story of Albert Einstein discovering relativity and equating energy, mass, and light in the most famous and elegant formula in all of science, $E = mc^2$; like the intelligence behind all of these achievements brings sheer mental delight to the enlightened minds of enthralled students—how much more will we delight to learn in heaven how God's wise plan utilized the most irrational motions of sin to complete such evident glory. There is a reason for absolutely everything. And those reasons will be delightful to study.

J. I. Packer's Train Station Analogy Completed

In a chapter entitled "God's Wisdom and Ours" in his classic book *Knowing God*, J. I. Packer considers the kind of wisdom God gives on earth. Packer tempers our expectations to protect us from unhealthy speculations. He uses an analogy from the York train station, one of the busiest terminals in England. If you were to watch the trains coming and going, you might be bewildered with many of the trains' actions. However, if you were in the control center high above the platform, you could see the master panel with all the lines coming in and out of the station; there the stationmaster can control the flow. You would understand why this train was stopped for five minutes, that one was diverted to a side rail for an hour, and others were allowed to proceed. All of the movements would become clearer to you once you saw the control panel and had the explanation from the station-master. But then, Packer adds,

> Now, the mistake that is commonly made is to suppose that this is an illustration of what God does when he bestows wisdom. . . . People feel if they were really walking close to God, so that he could impart wisdom to them freely, then

they would, so to speak, find themselves in the signal-box; they would discern the real purpose of everything that happened to them, and it would be clear to them every moment how God was making all things work together for good.[17]

Packer properly lowers our expectations for earthly insight. We are never invited up into the heavenly realms for perspective on the "mystery of providence." As Paul said, "Oh, the depth of the riches and wisdom and knowledge of God! How unsearchable are his judgments and how inscrutable his ways!" (Rom. 11:33). Instead of detailed inside information, Packer says God gives theological principles—rules of the road—by which we can navigate the twists and turns on the complex and winding road of providence. At the end of the chapter, Packer completes his meditation with these words: "Let us see to it, then, that . . . we do not frustrate the wise purpose of God by neglecting faith and faithfulness in order to pursue a kind of knowledge which in this world it is not given to us to have."[18] But note the phrase "in this world"! Packer didn't address the *eternal world*, the heavenly one, where God will invite us into the signal-box for a retrospective view of his wise ways in this present age.

God Is His Own Interpreter

William Cowper, an eighteenth-century English hymnwriter, battled depression for most of his life. His most famous hymn is known by its first line:

> God moves in a mysterious way,
> His wonders to perform;

He plants his footsteps in the sea,
And rides upon the storm.

Deep in unfathomable mines
Of never failing skill;
He treasures up his bright designs,
And works his sovereign will.

Ye fearful saints fresh courage take,
The clouds ye so much dread
Are big with mercy, and shall break
In blessings on your head.

Blind unbelief is sure to err,
And scan his work in vain;
God is his own interpreter,
And he will make it plain.[19]

Look carefully at the last stanza: "God is his own interpreter, and he will make it plain." God will interpret his own works, however peculiar and mysterious they seem to us when we experience them. And he will make plain each detail and what it accomplished in his overall perfect plan. But *when* will he do that? Certainly not here on earth. God did not tell Job about the challenge issued by Satan, nor why all ten of his children died. We know more of those details now than Job did then. But we cannot possibly believe we know more now than Job knows in heaven or what we will know for all eternity when God gives his full interpretation for all the elect. "He will make it plain."

CHAPTER 13

Memories of the Damned

We come now to two very weighty questions in our study of heavenly memories: Will the redeemed in heaven be fully aware of the damned in hell—who they were in life, and what they will be suffering eternally? Will the damned in hell remember their earthly lives while they are suffering hell's torments? I believe the answer to both questions is yes. And I believe this knowledge is part of the full experience of salvation for the redeemed and of condemnation for the damned.

As we contemplate the harder aspects of heavenly memory, we must ever keep before us the promise of eternal happiness in Revelation 21:4: "He will wipe away every tear from their eyes, and death shall be no more, neither shall there be mourning, nor crying, nor pain anymore, for the former things have passed away." This is an eternity completely free from all forms of pain, including mental anguish. But it is hard for us to imagine being eternally happy in heaven while the majority of humanity is suffering eternal conscious torment in hell. This is made even more difficult if we are aware of people we loved in this world who are in anguish eternally, which is why some conclude that we will be completely ignorant of the damned.

However, Scripture reveals that the redeemed in heaven will be completely aware of the damned. Therefore, they will actually have a fuller sense of their history and their just punishment. But this knowledge will cause the redeemed no pain. This will be true even of those we deeply love in this world—a dear spouse, a beloved parent, a precious child. There will be no mourning, for if there were, it would be as if we were suffering torments with them and would directly violate the promise of Revelation 21:4.

The Rich Man and Lazarus

Christ's parable of the rich man and Lazarus (Luke 16:19–31) tells about Lazarus in heaven with Father Abraham while the unnamed rich man is in torment in hell. Abraham knows where this man is, knows what he is suffering and why, and can even have conversation with him. Since he calls the rich man "child" in verse 25, just as he calls Abraham "father," their earthly relationship is remembered by both. That Lazarus is at Abraham's side implies that he has as clear a view of the rich man's agonies as Abraham does. Abraham said to the rich man, "You are in anguish," and recounts the good things the man had in his life, while Lazarus had nothing good. The rich man's indifference to Lazarus's suffering epitomizes his selfish life. It is obvious that Abraham does not see his sentence as unjust in any way. The rich man looks up and sees both Abraham and Lazarus in comfort, greatly increasing his anguish and regret. That grief is compounded by Abraham's command to the rich man that he "remember" how it was for him in life. The damned do remember (and have eternal cause to regret) their actions in life. The rich man remembers his family members, who continue to live faithless lives. This parable helps us to see that the redeemed in heaven are fully aware of the damned in hell and their identity, while the damned in hell are fully aware of their past lives and the present delights of heaven.

God's Justice on Eternal Display

Revelation 14:9–11 is one of the key Scriptures on the eternal, conscious torment of the damned, for it says "the smoke of their torment goes up forever and ever," with "no rest day or night." It also says they will be tormented "in the presence of the holy angels and in the presence of the Lamb." The Lamb, Jesus Christ, looks on their anguish, not in any way ashamed of the righteous punishment of God's wrath meted out full strength. And neither are the holy angels, who stand with the Lamb justifying the justice of God. As they do also in Revelation 16:

> "Just are you, O Holy One, who is and who was,
>   for you brought these judgments.
> For they have shed the blood of saints and prophets,
>   and you have given them blood to drink.
> It is what they deserve!"

And I heard the altar saying,

> "Yes, Lord God the Almighty,
>   true and just are your judgments!" (vv. 5–7)

The angel knows the specific crimes the wicked of the earth have committed against the people of God, and how the punishment truly fits the crimes. Now, if Jesus and the angels are aware of the sins of the damned and the justice of God's wrath outpoured, it is very reasonable to assume the redeemed in heaven are aware as well. Why would God hide it from them? He is telling us now in the Scripture that it will happen. How much more will we be able to look on it with resurrected eyes and worship God's justice in it with resurrected hearts?

The final statement in the book of Isaiah describes life in the new heaven and new earth:

> And they shall go out and look on the dead bodies of the men who have rebelled against me. For their worm shall not die, their fire shall not be quenched, and they shall be an abhorrence to all flesh. (Isa. 66:24)

Isaiah's prophecy ends with a description of hell. This is the very verse Jesus quotes when describing the torments of hell (Mark 9:47–48). We will "look on the dead bodies of the men who have rebelled" against God, who are in eternal torment in hell. God will not hide it from us. We will be completely conformed to Christ, able to handle the whole truth. And as we look on the bodies of the damned, we will know that they rebelled against God. God's perfect justice will be eternally vindicated before us.

Present Anguish Replaced by Heavenly Worship

I understand how difficult this is for us to handle. That is as it should be. The grief we feel about the spiritual condition of the lost is completely appropriate while there is still time for them to repent and come to Christ. Jesus wept over Jerusalem (Luke 19:41–42). Paul had "great sorrow and unceasing anguish" in his heart for lost Jews (Rom. 9:2). The Holy Spirit has used this holy agony in every generation to motivate missionaries to make extreme exertions to win lost people to Christ. Even the most hardened sinners can repent and find salvation through faith in Christ before they die. We should pour out tears and labor as tirelessly as Paul did to win lost people.

But after judgment day, the "day of salvation" will have ended forever (2 Cor. 6:2). And when it comes to loved ones, in heaven our priority structure will be eternally conformed to Christ's words: "Anyone who loves their father or mother more than me is not worthy of me; anyone who loves their son or daughter more than me is not worthy of me" (Matt. 10:37 NIV). In the same way, God commanded all the Israelites to show greater loyalty to him than to any loved one, especially if that loved one was luring them to follow other gods (Deut. 13:6–10). How much more will this be the standard for all eternity concerning any family member, friend, or neighbor who refused to follow Christ? We will be totally consumed with the glory of God and see unrepentant sin and rebellion against him as the utterly wicked things they are.

Charles Spurgeon's mother prayed for him while he was an unconverted teenager. She poured out prayers and tears for him to be saved, yearning to lead him to Christ. Spurgeon recounts,

> I cannot tell how much I owe to the solemn words of my good mother. . . . I remember on one occasion her praying thus:

181

"Now, Lord, if my children go on in their sins, it will not be from ignorance that they perish, and my soul must bear a swift witness against them at the day of judgment if they lay not hold of Christ." That thought of my mother's bearing a swift witness against me pierced my conscience. . . . How can I ever forget when she bowed her knee, and with her arms about my neck, prayed, "Oh, that my son might live before Thee!"[1]

This godly woman had the faith and courage to get it right. She did everything she could to lead her son to Christ, but if he refused, she would heartily testify against him on judgment day in her surpassing loyalty to Christ.

Moreover, in hell the lost people we loved on earth will have been stripped of every common grace blessing that made them attractive to us. The kindly agnostic grandmother who baked delicious oatmeal raisin cookies; the worldly businessman who consistently donated large sums to charity; the college roommate who told hilarious stories and was fun to watch a football game with; our own unbelieving mother who loved us sacrificially and cared for us every day of our lives; our precious unbelieving son who called every day and never forgot our birthday. These people may have loved us, but they never loved Jesus. And after judgment day, "every good and every perfect gift" that God ever gave to them (James 1:17) will be judicially taken from them, and they will become morally, spiritually, and physically repulsive. Filled with rage at God, unrepentant of their sins, they will think they do not deserve to be in hell (Rev. 9:20; 16:9, 11). The redeemed in heaven will have infinitely different feelings about the people they formerly loved. And they will wholeheartedly endorse God's justice in condemning them.

God's People Specifically Vindicated

This book focuses on *the heavenly memory of earthly history*. That the damned have a specific history of evil on earth is essential to God's justice in damning them. This history includes acts of injustice and the vicious persecution of the people of God. Cain's hatred of his righteous brother Abel is the paradigm for the children of the devil throughout the course of human history (1 John 3:12). And a major part of the book of Revelation is the assault by the Dragon and his human lackeys on the people of God, along with Christ's desire to defend his people and vindicate them (Rev. 16:6).

The consistent teaching of the New Testament is for Christians to turn the other cheek when slapped, to go the extra mile, and to "love your enemies and pray for those who persecute you" (Matt. 5:39–41, 44). Paul specifically forbids taking revenge on those who hurt us. But when saying this, he also reminds us that God will avenge us, if we entrust ourselves to him:

> Beloved, never avenge yourselves, but leave it to the wrath of God, for it is written, *"Vengeance is mine, I will repay*, says the Lord." To the contrary, "if your enemy is hungry, feed him; if he is thirsty, give him something to drink; for by so doing you will heap burning coals on his head." Do not be overcome by evil, but overcome evil with good. (Rom. 12:19–21)

The vicious attacks of your enemies should be overcome with acts of kindness and goodness. However, many hate-filled persecutors of Christians are never converted. That means they have an outstanding debt that will not be paid by the shed blood of Christ but only by the wrath of God. In Revelation 6, the martyrs in heaven cry out for vengeance against their persecutors:

> "O Sovereign Lord, holy and true, how long before you will judge and avenge our blood on those who dwell on the earth?" Then they were each given a white robe and told to rest a little longer, until the number of their fellow servants and their brothers should be complete, who were to be killed as they themselves had been. (vv. 10–11)

This is significant for our study, because it shows that heaven's inhabitants know three things: they were martyred, so they remember their own sufferings; they know their persecutors have not yet been judged, so they are aware of events on earth; their demand for vengeance is not ungodly.

Hell, therefore, is the fulfillment of God's pledge to avenge his saints. When God says, "Vengeance is mine; I will repay," he is making a promise to his people. Most of our enemies will not meet justice in this life. So the vindication of the saints and their suffering must be in eternity, and the saints should see it. We must know that particular people who did specifically evil things to us or our loved ones are suffering the wrath of God for their crimes. This is what Christ vowed in the parable of the persistent widow (Luke 18:1–8). The widow begs an unjust judge for justice against her enemies, and Jesus applies her story to us with these words: "And will not God give justice to his elect, who cry to him day and night? Will he delay long over them? I tell you, he will give justice to them speedily" (vv. 7–8). Think of the millions of

God's people over millennia of history who cried out for relief from some vicious persecutor and who were deeply troubled that God did not seem to grant their request for justice.

This truth is especially satisfying for those who suffered oppression in lives of slavery or under anti-Christian governments. Their persecutors seemed to "get away with murder." In Alexander Dumas's classic tale of revenge, *The Count of Monte Cristo*, Edmond Dantès is unjustly imprisoned. He argues that even execution by the law for certain crimes is insufficient vengeance.

> "Listen," said the count, and hatred mounted his face, as blood would in the face of any other. "If a man had by unheard-of and excruciating tortures destroyed your father, your mother, your mistress, that is, one of those beings who when they are torn from you, leave a desolation, a wound that never closes in your breast, do you think that society gives you justice by causing the blade of the guillotine to pass between the base of the occiput and the trapezal muscles of the murderer—by making he who has caused us years of moral sufferings undergo a few moments of physical pain?"[2]

In response, others ask if the count is advocating medieval torture, but he says even that is insufficient. The scriptural answer—eternal hell under the just wrath of God—does not enter the discussion.

God's Ultimate Purpose for the Damned

No passage delves into these questions more powerfully than Romans 9:18–24. In Romans 9–11, Paul is seeking to address the weighty question, Why are the Jews, God's chosen people, overwhelmingly rejecting the gospel of Jesus Christ? Paul's answer is multifaceted. In Romans 9, he begins by teaching the doctrine of individual election and reprobation. Individual people, both Jews and gentiles alike, are chosen by the sovereign will of God to be either believers or unbelievers. God "has mercy on whomever he wills, and he hardens whomever he wills" (Rom. 9:18). So, every person is either a "vessel of mercy" or a "vessel of wrath" (vv. 22–23). When we get to heaven, we will be surrounded by the "vessels of mercy," for Christ loses none of those that the Father has given him (John 6:39–40). But the "vessels of wrath" God willed to harden, and every one of them is justly condemned. There is a long history of rancorous debate on these issues, but in heaven, there will be no debate. What God did with every vessel of mercy and vessel of wrath will be perfectly unveiled by that time.

But thoughtful people who read Romans 9 will ask, "Why does God even create the human beings who will be vessels of wrath?" Jesus himself said of Judas the betrayer, "It would have been better for that man if he had not been born" (Matt. 26:24). So why was Judas born? Paul raised and answered that very question in Romans 9:20–24. He asserted God's rights as a potter to make out of the same lump of clay vessels for different purposes (v. 21). Then he said,

> What if God, desiring to show his wrath and to make known his power, has endured with much patience vessels of wrath prepared for destruction, in order to make known the riches of his glory for vessels of mercy, which he has prepared beforehand for glory[?] (vv. 22–23)

God brings people into the world knowing they will be vessels of wrath. His purpose for them is to display three of his attributes: wrath, power, and patience. The ultimate purpose of these vessels of wrath is to make known the riches of his glory and mercy to his vessels of mercy, who are being prepared for glory. Paul uses two verbs in verses 22–23 that speak of a demonstration or education concerning his nature: *endeknumi*, "to put on display," and *gnoridzo*, "to make known." This is the essence of glory: the radiant display of God's attributes. God creates individuals who will eventually end up in hell to put his attributes on display: wrath, power, and patience toward the reprobate; mercy and glory toward the elect.

When does God make this revelation of his attributes? Some of that demonstration happens here on earth, as the gospel is preached. The elect understand by faith what is happening around them every day, and where this is all heading. But it also takes faith to see that God is exhibiting his wrath by giving the reprobate over to their sins. It does not seem like wrath at the time, for the wicked are simply doing what they want to do. The completed presentation of God's wrath must take place in eternity.

Why is this? First, because we don't know who the reprobate are in this world. That is one thing we absolutely *cannot* know now, for the unconverted elect look exactly like the unconverted non-elect in this world. Saul of Tarsus was breathing threats and murder against the Lord's disciples the very morning he was converted (Acts 9:1).

Second, Romans 9:22 says that God "has endured with much patience" these vessels of wrath. While they lived, there was little to no sign of wrath. Some exceedingly wicked people may have viciously persecuted Christ's people, gained immense wealth and power, lived lives of indolence and luxury, had healthy bodies fit through exercise and an excellent diet, and died at an old age surrounded by their doting families. Job details this in Job 21:7–13. *When* did God display his justice in their cases? It wasn't in this world!

Finally, God's wrath against the wicked is almost always spoken of as occurring in hell, not suffering on earth. As Jesus said, "Do not fear those who kill the body but cannot kill the soul. Rather fear him who can destroy both soul and body in hell" (Matt. 10:28). And Romans 2:5–11 says the wicked store up wrath against themselves every day of their lives in the record books of God. Those books will be opened "on the day of wrath when God's righteous judgment will be revealed" (v. 5). That is judgment day. But even judgment day's legal verdict is not the ultimate exhibition of God's wrath and power; only hell will perfectly display those attributes. And only in heaven will we finally see the history of how incredibly patient he was with the wicked. Only then will we realize how intensely provocative the sins of the human race were to the holiness of God, and how day after day, year after year, God "spread out [his] hands to a disobedient and defiant people" (10:21 HCSB). Also, by seeing and understanding the just wrath of God against sinners in hell, the redeemed will understand the full meaning of God's grace toward them. We will plumb the depths of this truth: "There but for the grace of God go I."

The "display" language is key here, for the reprobate exist to make all these attributes of God radiantly glorious to the elect. If in heaven the redeemed have no knowledge of the damned in hell, God's purpose in Romans 9 is never really fulfilled.

What the Damned Will Remember

The final aspect of this sobering meditation is to consider the memory of the damned as they experience eternal conscious torment. We have already reminded ourselves of the unchangeable bliss of heaven: no death, mourning, crying, or pain (Rev. 21:4). But the exact opposite is true of hell. For eternity, the damned will be immersed in nothing but death, mourning, crying, and pain. They will be forever dying, such that hell is spoken of as "the second death" but also as the place where the "worm does not die" (20:14; Mark 9:48). There will be "weeping and gnashing of teeth" (Matt. 8:12), implying immeasurable psychological and emotional anguish. And the memories of the damned will fuel this anguish.

Remembering Wasted Gospel Opportunities

Of all the memories that will torment the damned the most, it will be the opportunities many of them had in life to hear the gospel faithfully proclaimed. Hundreds of millions of the damned heard the gospel repeatedly in their lives. And they will have eternal cause to regret casting aside the free offer of salvation.

On January 27, 1820, Adoniram Judson, during his missionary work in Burma, traveled to the royal city of Ava with his coworker, James Colman, seeking to secure an audience with the ruler of Burma, King Bagyidaw. Judson intended to request permission to preach the gospel in Burma, but his deepest desire was to lead the king to faith in Christ. Escorted into an ornate audience room, Judson and Colman waited with great anticipation to meet the king. Suddenly every Burman in the room threw himself to the floor because "the Golden Feet had entered the room." The king had arrived. Courtney Anderson's description of this moment is powerful:

> The man who strode unattended toward them with the proud gait and majesty of an Eastern monarch . . . was impressive on account of his rank rather than his stature or costume. . . . As he drew near, he caught sight of the two kneeling missionaries, the only people in the room who dared look at him and were not stretched flat on the floor.
>
> [Judson and Colman began to explain their purpose to the king.] The king listened quietly. Then he stretched out his hand. Maung Zah [a royal official] crawled forward and presented the petition. His Majesty took it and deliberately read it through, from top to bottom. Meanwhile, Adoniram passed to Maung Zah a carefully abridged and edited copy of the [gospel] tract which Adoniram had written four years before. When the king had finished the petition, he silently returned it to Maung Zah, who now handed him the tract. Watching the king take the tract, Adoniram prayed inwardly with all the fervor of his heart, "Oh, have mercy on Burma! Have mercy on her king!"
>
> But King Bagyidaw merely read the opening sentences: "There is one Being who exists eternally; who is exempt from sickness, old age, and death; who is, and was, and will be, without beginning and without end. Besides this, the true God, there is no other God . . ." Then he opened his hand with indifference and let the paper fall to the floor.[3]

We do not know if King Bagyidaw ever came to faith in Christ. If he did not, I believe he will eternally see this interaction with Judson from an entirely different point of view. He thought he was receiving an impertinent and disrespectful foreigner begging to spread his religion among his subjects. In reality, the true King of kings and Lord of lords was giving this mortal sinner an opportunity to repent of his rebellion and receive the gift of eternal life in the kingdom of God. Instead, he let the invitation slip from his fingers and drop from his attention. How eternally filled with regret he will be when he sees that moment for what it was! What would he "give in return for his soul"? (Matt. 16:26). What of his wealth would not he trade for another chance to talk with Adoniram Judson? But he possesses nothing in hell. And the moment has passed forever. God calls to all sinners now, "Seek the LORD while he may be found; call upon him while he is near" (Isa. 55:6). "Behold, now is the favorable time; behold, now is the day of salvation" (2 Cor. 6:2).

CHAPTER 14

The Consummation of Our Education in Evil

A dam and Eve stood before the forbidden tree in the garden of Eden, little knowing that the future of humanity hung in the balance. The tree had an evocative name: the "tree of the knowledge of good and evil." The serpent clinched his temptation with these words: "God knows that when you eat of it your eyes will be opened, and you will be like God, *knowing good and evil*" (Gen. 3:5). Eve yearned for this knowledge, for the fruit had power to make her wise like God. So "she took of its fruit and ate, and she also gave some to her husband who was with her, and he ate" (v. 6). Suddenly "the eyes of both were opened" (v. 7) and their education in evil began.

This education has been infinitely costly. God confirmed it had begun when he repeated the words the serpent had said: "Behold, the man has become like one of us in knowing good and evil" (v. 22). Even looking ahead to the great sacrifice that would be necessary to crush the serpent's head, God chose that history should unfold from that point, rather than shutting it down immediately. This choice reflects the grace of God, and it was bought by the blood of Christ. But essential to that history is the education Adam sought on behalf of his descendants, matriculation in the university of good and evil.

If in heaven, the facts and details of that education are forgotten, wiped clean by the hand of God, then what was the point of it all? God will be glorified in heaven by the review of his earthly purposes and deeds, but he will be even more glorified when we are totally conformed to his Son, our Lord Jesus Christ. And that will require eternal memory of evil.

Conformed to the Image of Christ

God's plan for the salvation of his elect is revealed in these words: "For those whom he foreknew he also predestined to be *conformed to the image of his Son*, in order that he might be the firstborn among many brothers" (Rom. 8:29). God will be perfectly glorified in the redeemed in heaven because they will all be perfectly conformed to Christ. God originally created humanity to be in his image and likeness (Gen. 1:26–27), and the gospel redeems people to be "created after the likeness of God in true righteousness and holiness" (Eph. 4:24).

Part of Christ's glory is described magnificently in Hebrews 1:9, in which God the Father says to his only begotten Son, "You have loved righteousness and hated wickedness." This is the foundation of his eternal throne, and in heaven his glory will shine more brightly than we can possibly imagine.

Every one of his redeemed will be conformed to him in this respect: we also will love righteousness and hate wickedness. Just as the psalmist commanded us, "O you who love the LORD, hate evil!" (Ps. 97:10).

But how would we be able to hate something we know nothing about? If in heaven our memories of evil are completely erased, our basis for hating evil would be eliminated as well. To be like God, to be conformed to Christ, we must have an accurate knowledge of evil and see it for what it really is, and then hate it with every fiber of our being. Our education in evil will be made complete in heaven's eternal history lessons.

That Sin Might Be Displayed as "Utterly Sinful"

One of God's purposes in redemptive history was using his law to draw out the true nature of evil and display it for his chosen people. Paul tells us that the law came that Adam's trespass might *increase* (Rom. 5:20). At first glance, this seems illogical, given God's holy hatred of sin. One might think that the effect of the introduction of God's holy law would be to restrain evil in us and keep it from spreading. But Paul says exactly the opposite. Similarly, two chapters later he recounts the way sin hijacked the command of God, "You shall not covet," and used it to produce covetous desires inside his heart. Sin somehow twisted a perfectly holy, righteous, and good command (7:7–11) and used it to produce an evil result in a human heart. This in no way surprised God. Rather, it was exactly what the law of God was intended to do: exhibit evil for the elect. As Paul writes, "in order that sin might be *shown* to be sin, and through the commandment might become sinful beyond measure" (v. 13) or "utterly sinful" (v. 13 NASB). God will employ his perfect review of earth's history—the history of evil—to complete our education and help us to see sin as sinful beyond any dimensions we could possibly have measured.

We Can't Handle the Full Disclosure . . . Yet

But the full revelation of the nature of evil will never occur in this world, because we could not handle it. This is why God clothed Adam and Eve with animal skins, and why he conceals most sins from public view, even when we are addressing sin in the life of the church. In Matthew 18:15, Christ commands us to confront someone who has sinned against us "in private" (NASB). He desires as few people know about the sin as possible. Christ said, "I still have many things to say to you, but you cannot bear them now" (John 16:12). So it is with evil, for there is only so much we can handle, and a fuller disclosure while we are still battling with internal lusts would only tempt us more and do us harm. Even if it did not tempt us, it would overwhelm us with dismay at the magnitude of its power. But in heaven, we will be glorified in soul as well as body and will be able to handle the full disclosure of the truth. And that full disclosure of the career of evil over the span of redemptive history will feed our hatred of it, thus deepening our conformity to Christ.

When I was growing up, I remember the "creature feature" movies that played on TV on Saturday afternoons. The most memorable was *Godzilla*, a massive reptile concocted by Japanese film producers. At a climactic point in the movie, the monster stood up in the harbor, terrifying the people of Tokyo. Seeing his immensity inevitably sent them running and screaming, hoping to escape imminent destruction. In a metaphorical sense, I can picture God in heaven pulling the vile monster Evil out of the dark harbor that had concealed its true size. He holds it by its disgusting head as it drips filthy residue, saying, "Behold, my children, the full magnitude and nature of evil! Look upon it now and hate it as I do!" In glory, we will be prepared to receive this revelation.

Tracing Out the Grand Narrative of Evil

The unfolding history of evil from that first sin at Eden's tree is essentially the story of redemption, told in every book of the Bible and on almost every page. Therefore, I cannot trace it out here with any detail. Instead, it will be the task of God our heavenly history teacher to do it as fully as he deems necessary.

First, we will fully realize in heaven how stubborn and relentless sin was in every era of redemptive history. We will see just how difficult this virus was to eradicate, how prone it was to resurface and metastasize. Sin began with Adam and Eve eating a piece of fruit. By the next chapter, it grew to include Cain's murder of his brother. Quickly, it spread to a corruption of marriage and a cold-blooded murder by the first tyrant, Lamech (Gen. 4:23). By the time of Noah, evil had spread to such a degree that "man's wickedness was widespread on the earth and that every scheme his mind thought of was nothing but evil all the time" (6:5 HCSB). This prompted the worldwide flood, temporarily cleansing the earth of the filth of human sin.

But it did not rid us of the virus. "Sin reigned" (Rom. 5:21) from Noah to Abraham, from Abraham to Moses, and from Moses to Christ. The old covenant only put sin on display in the history of the nation of Israel. The law of Moses had no solution to the sin problem—it just defined it and exposed it.

Then God made a new covenant in the blood of his Son, Jesus Christ. By the terms of this new covenant, sin is actually forgiven and our sinful natures are transformed; God wrote his laws in our minds and on our hearts (Heb. 8:10–12). But indwelling sin remained, and the mysterious combination of the Holy Spirit's activity and human activity in sanctification has resulted in a tragically mixed record of Christians sometimes sinning and sometimes acting righteously. This bizarre mixture of partial obedience and partial disobedience has stained every day of church history. It has hindered the spread of the gospel from Jerusalem through Judea and Samaria and to the ends of the earth. It has resulted in church divisions and factions, power struggles between strong leaders, occasional wandering from the pure truth of the Word, and a tragically meandering path of progress in every century up to this present day. The three powerful enemies of each Christian—the world, the flesh, and the devil—wreak havoc in the lives of Christians, resulting in sinful marriages, sinful parenting, sinful churches, and sinful citizenship, contaminating everything. Only by God's sovereign grace will the plan of redemption reach its consummation in the salvation of every person elected by God from before the foundation of the world. Sin is the constant, resilient enemy of that amazing plan, and heaven's education alone will show the dimensions and details of its deadly power.

A Heavenly "Center for Disease Prevention"

The Centers for Disease Control and Prevention, or CDC, is housed in a sleek steel and glass building in Atlanta. Despite its attractive outward appearance, it contains a shop of horrors. For research purposes, active samples of viruses and bacteria are stored there. These organisms have caused some of the deadliest diseases in human experience, including Ebola, HIV, the Marburg virus, and more recently, COVID-19. Of all these microscopic villains, none has a more devastating record of delivering death than the *variola* virus that causes smallpox. There have been countless smallpox epidemics over history: one ravaged Rome for fifteen years beginning in AD 165, killing as many as five million people and greatly weakening the Roman Empire. Smallpox was inadvertently brought to the Aztec population by the Spanish conquistadors, enabling Hernan Cortez to topple the mighty Aztec empire with a handful of men. It was perhaps the greatest killer of the twentieth century, claiming anywhere from three hundred to five hundred million people.[1]

Medical science has not developed a cure for smallpox. However, concerted efforts at worldwide vaccination proved so effective that in December 1979, the World Health Organization declared smallpox to have been eradicated from the face of the earth. The only known samples of the *variola* virus on earth are kept in the CDC in Atlanta and in a similar facility near Moscow. Why not destroy those samples? The CDC states that all their deadly samples are for one purpose: research for the future protection of the human race. Scientists at the CDC can access these samples any time to study their properties and then use that knowledge to heal sick people and prevent the spread of similar infectious diseases.

In the same way, God's stockpile of the specific patterns of sin across every generation of human history may be essential to prevent the spread of sin from ever happening again. If all memory of sin is lost in heaven, not only will we not be able to hate wickedness like Jesus does but we will also be more vulnerable to a future outbreak. When we see the list of sins in certain places in Scripture, we could liken them to the samples the CDC keeps in its labs:

> Sexual immorality, impurity, sensuality, idolatry, sorcery, enmity, strife, jealousy, fits of anger, rivalries, dissensions, divisions, envy, drunkenness, orgies, and things like these. (Gal. 5:19–21)

> They were filled with all manner of unrighteousness, evil, covetousness, malice . . . envy, murder, strife, deceit, maliciousness. They are gossips, slanderers, haters of God, insolent, haughty, boastful, inventors of evil, disobedient to parents, foolish, faithless, heartless, ruthless. (Rom. 1:29–31)

> People will be lovers of self, lovers of money, proud, arrogant, abusive, disobedient to their parents, ungrateful, unholy, heartless, unappeasable, slanderous, without self-control, brutal, not loving good, treacherous, reckless, swollen with conceit, lovers of pleasure rather than lovers of God, having the appearance of godliness, but denying its power. (2 Tim. 3:2–5)

Each of these sinful demeanors or actions has a long history. Those histories must not be lost, lest the inhabitants of heaven forget their virulent nature and become susceptible again. In this way, heaven will be its own laboratory of the science of sin and its only remedy: the grace of God in Jesus Christ.

"Never Again": The Somber Lessons of the Holocaust Museum

Another analogy comes from one of my most sobering experiences: visiting the Holocaust Museum in Washington, DC. It is a vast, carefully detailed and assembled collection of historical artifacts, testimonies, photographs, and archived footage depicting the loss of the lives of over six million Jews, as well as many other people the Nazis hated. I will always remember what it was like to stand in one of the actual cattle cars that carried people to the concentration camps. I could feel the terror rising within my heart as I imagined what it would be like to be crowded into such a dark conveyance carrying me to my death. Perhaps the most affecting sight by far, however, was the pile of baby shoes confiscated by SS guards from their tiny victims.

The entire museum has one central purpose, summed up in two words: "Never again." This slogan is also emblazoned in five languages on an international monument at Dachau, one of the worst of the Nazi concentration camps.[2] It presses the need for continual education about the Jewish Holocaust in World War II in order to prevent genocide from happening anywhere else in the world at any time in the future.[3] It reminds me of Santayana's famous dictum: "Those who cannot remember the past are condemned to repeat it."[4]

Though many today may fervently hope for "never again," their desire is not much different from the hopeful name first given to World War I, "the War to End All Wars." The most devastating war in history, to date, followed only twenty years later. And since the Holocaust ended in 1945, there have been numerous state-sponsored genocides resulting in millions of deaths, including the horrific "killing fields" of Cambodia. While sin continues its hideous march across the face of the globe, leaving its bloody footprints on every page of history, no amount of education will stop it. Only the sovereign grace of God consummated in heaven will finally stop all wars, all genocides, and all other manifestations of evil.

If heaven will contain a wise display of the history of evil over six thousand years, I believe that eternal knowledge in our glorified hearts will help prevent any future fall into the sin Satan started before humanity was ever created. Once we are in heaven, either a future repeat of rebellion, evil, and sin will happen or it won't. But if a future fall from heavenly glory is possible, then how could these verses be fulfilled?

> I am the resurrection and the life; the one who believes in me will live, even though he dies, and everyone who lives and believes in Me *will never die.* (John 11:25–26 NASB)

> Surely goodness and love shall follow me all the days of my life, and *I shall dwell in the house of the* LORD *forever.* (Ps. 23:6)

> No longer will violence be heard in your land,
> nor ruin or destruction within your borders,

but you will call your walls Salvation
    and your gates Praise.
The sun will no more be your light by day,
    nor will the brightness of the moon shine on you,
for the Lord will be your everlasting light,
    and your God will be your glory.
Your sun will never set again,
    and your moon will wane no more;
the Lord will be your everlasting light,
    and your days of sorrow will end.
Then will all your people be righteous
    and they will possess the land forever. (Isa. 60:18–21 NIV)

Those who are wise will shine like the brightness of the heavens, and those who lead many to righteousness, like the stars *for ever and ever.* (Dan. 12:3 NIV)

There will be no more night. They will not need the light of a lamp or the light of the sun, for the Lord God will give them light. *And they will reign for ever and ever.* (Rev. 22:5 NIV)

If we will remember the past history of evil, and if we will never again fall into evil, either those two facts will be connected or they won't. It seems more likely that they are causally connected: because we will know the whole history of evil and its detailed nature, and because we are perfectly conformed in heart to Christ, we will hate it perfectly. Therefore, the glorified saints in heaven will never again fall into sin for two vital reasons: (1) they understand and love the glory of God in all its dimensions; (2) they understand and hate wickedness in all its dimensions.

Eternally Destroying Curiosity for Evil

If all of the redeemed have a memory wipe after judgment day and enter heaven forgetting all of redemptive history, we will have no knowledge whatsoever of evil. But evil would still exist in hell, for damnation will not transform Satan, demons, or damned humans. They will still be rebels, seething in rage. And would that not stand as an eternal temptation to the ignorant redeemed?

Some years ago, I heard an *Arabian Nights* story that made a powerful impression on me. It is called "The Man Who Never Laughed Again to the End of His Days."[5] Here is a quick summary:

> A young man is recruited to care for a number of older men in a mansion. They all spend their entire days weeping, though the young man is forbidden from asking why. One by one, these older men all die till just one is left. The young man begs to know why they all spent their days in constant lamentation. With his dying breath, this old man divulges that there is a door in the garden through which he must never pass. But if he goes through that door, he will learn the dark secret. Out of love for the young man, the dying man begs him not to. After the man dies, the young man is tormented by the allure of that door, held back only by the warning never to pass through it. Finally, his curiosity overcomes him, and he ventures through. He travels through a long corridor to a distant beach, where begins a series of adventures leading him to a luxurious life, married to a beautiful woman and ruling a prosperous kingdom.
>
> However, in that perfect kingdom he is shown another door in a garden and is warned not to go through it or he will

"repent when repentance will do him no good." He reasons with himself, "Look at what happened when I went through the door in the original garden. Perhaps an even more wonderful life awaits me beyond this door as well." So one day, unable to resist satisfying his curiosity, he passes through the forbidden door—and instantly regrets it. He is carried by a huge, fierce-looking eagle back to the original beach, and can never return to his paradise again. So he spends the rest of his life in the original garden weeping for his foolish curiosity and poisonous discontentment.

As I consider that story, I reflect on the parallel to what heaven would be like if evil still existed but we had no memory of its history over these six thousand years. Instead, we could well imagine metaphorically a forbidden doorway leading to a passageway of a new history of rebellion against almighty God. We would effectively be back at Eden with the same choice. With no memory, no history from which to know and hate wickedness, how could we be assured that we would not out of curiosity desire to open that forbidden door? But if we are eternally educated by God about the nature and history of evil, are transformed perfectly into the image of his Son, and love righteousness and hate wickedness, a future fall from heaven will be impossible.

CHAPTER 15

Applications

How Much Heaven Do You Want?

In the fall of 1722, the teenaged Jonathan Edwards wrote down a set of spiritual resolutions that would govern the way he would live for the rest of his life. Resolution #22 arrests my attention:

> Resolved, to endeavor to obtain for myself as much happiness, in the other world, as I possibly can, with all the power, might, vigor, and vehemence, yea violence, I am capable of, or can bring myself to exert, in any way that can be thought of.[1]

Based on all we have studied in this book, I commend this resolution to you as well. Edwards's foundational assumptions are breathtaking. One, there are gradations of happiness in heaven. (As we saw from our earlier study on his "Heaven Is a World of Love," "Every saint will be perfectly happy, but not equally happy."[2]). Two, how we live our lives in this world affects our level of happiness in heaven. And three, heavenly happiness is worth the most extreme mental and physical effort we can possibly exert in this world. I believe all three of those assumptions are biblical. I also believe that each Christian should embrace them and would find them immensely helpful both in this world and the next. I want to press these themes on our hearts now, to maximize our eternal experience of glory.

How Much Land Does a Man Need?

In 1886, Russian writer Leo Tolstoy wrote a short story entitled "How Much Land Does a Man Need?"[3] It was a warning against the deadly danger of worldly greed. Here is my quick summary:

> The story is set in Czarist Russia and focuses on a discontented man named Pahom. He believes that all his problems would be solved if he could just get enough land of his own. He makes a foolish boast: "If I had plenty of land, I wouldn't fear the devil himself!" But the devil hears him and determines his strategy: "I will give you land enough, and by that means get you into my power."
>
> The next several years, Pahom makes various efforts to gain more land. But no matter what he does, there is always some significant problem with the arrangement, resulting in more and more frustration for Pahom.
>
> Finally, he hears from a traveling merchant of a distant land where the Bashkir tribe lives. They have huge amounts of rich land located alongside a river that they are apparently willing to sell for pennies per acre. Pahom asks many questions and becomes convinced it is true. He scrapes together

all the money he has in the world, one thousand rubles, and travels hundreds of miles to the land of the Bashkirs.

Pahom introduces himself to the tribe and sits down with their leaders and their chieftain. He gives them gifts and drinks tea with them, and they tell him they like him very much. He then tells them he wants to buy some of their land, and they are delighted. When Pahom asks what the price is, he receives this cryptic answer: "Our price is always the same: one thousand rubles per day." Pahom does not understand. "How many acres is that?" They reply, "We do not know. We sell it by the day. As much land as you can go round on your feet in a day will be yours, and the price is one thousand rubles per day." "But in a day, a man can walk round a huge tract of land!" Pahom says. The chieftain laughs. "It will all be yours. But there is one condition: if you don't return on the same day to the spot where you started, your money is lost, and you get nothing." Pahom then asks, "How will I mark the boundaries of my land?" They tell him to take a spade and dig holes as he goes, piling up the dirt as markers. Later, they will plow from hole to hole. But they remind him, "You must return before the sun sets to the place where you started." Pahom agrees.

That night, Pahom is so excited he can't sleep for hours. He dreams of the wealthy life awaiting him after he gains such a huge tract of land. He reasons, "I can easily go thirty-five miles in a day, especially since it is the summer and the days are long. Within a thirty-five-mile boundary, what a lot of land I will have!" He makes plans to buy a team of oxen, to rent some of the land out to tenant farmers, to sell some of the worst land for capital. Finally, he dozes off . . . but has a weird dream of someone laughing just outside his tent. In the dream, it turns out to be the devil laughing at him. And in the final part of the dream, he sees himself lying dead on the ground.

When he can sleep no longer, he rouses the Bashkir leaders and tells them he is eager to start, even before the sun comes up. They ascend a high hill that overlooks the whole region. The chieftain places his cap on the ground as both his starting and ending place. And soon, Pahom is off to make his life's fortune.

He decides to travel east and goes at a brisk but steady pace. He can't believe how rich the soil is and how beautiful the countryside. When he had gone about three miles, he digs a hole and piles up the dirt. He looks back at the hill where he'd started, and it seems quite distant. The day is becoming hotter and hotter, and Pahom takes off his overcoat and boots so he can travel more easily. The land only gets richer and richer as he goes on. He decides to travel for three more miles before digging another hole and turning left, and the walking is still going very well. He is about to dig another hole and turn left to start back toward the starting hill when he notices a well-watered tract just beyond himself. It would be a shame to leave it out, so he pushes himself a little further to include it. He digs his hole and then turns left toward the hill. But it looks very distant, and the people on it look like tiny ants. By now it is well past noon and the sun seems to be going faster and faster across the sky. Pahom's legs are heavy, his lungs are burning, and he begins to be in significant pain. He decides to make the third leg much shorter, fearful that he has seriously overextended himself. All he wants to do now is get back to the hill as quickly as possible, but it is still quite distant. Though walking is now a great difficulty, he quickens his pace. A paralyzing fear rises in his heart that he will lose everything because of his ambition. So he begins to run, racing the sun as it accelerates toward the horizon. His pants and shirt are soaked with sweat, his heart pounds in his chest like a blacksmith's hammer, and his legs feel like they are made of wood. He is increasingly fearful that he will die, but he presses on.

As he reaches the bottom of the hill at last, he can hear the Bashkirs cheering him on. But just at that moment, the sun dips below the horizon and the ground around him grows dark. He collapses in agony and grief to the ground, convinced he has lost everything. But the Bashkirs call to him from the top of the hill, saying they could still see the sun from up there. So he rouses himself for one massive final push up the hill. At the last possible moment, just before the sun dips below the horizon ending the day, he dives for the chieftain's cap and grasps it. The chieftain says, "What a fine fellow! He has gained much land!" But a stream of blood flows from Pahom's mouth, for he is dead!

The Bashkirs click their tongues to show pity. Then they pick up the spade he carried around the circuit and dig a grave for Pahom to lie in. Six feet from his head to his heels was all the land he needed.

Tolstoy's point is that we should beware this kind of worldly ambition. After I read that story, I realized it was a great sermon illustration for Jesus's warning "What will it profit a man if he gains the whole world and forfeits his soul?" (Matt. 16:26).

How Much Heaven Do You Want?

However, some years later I was pondering the significance of Jonathan Edwards's resolution to exert himself maximally for heavenly happiness. As I did, Tolstoy's story of relentless ambition took on a new light. I wondered if many Christians are not ambitious enough when it comes to laying claim to heavenly territory. If the story were seen in the light of storing up treasure in heaven, I picture some Christians as spiritual Pahoms in Bashkir land, sleeping in their tents as the sun rises. The Bashkir chieftain has to send some folks to the tent to see if Pahom still wants some land or not. Pahom awakes, rubs the sleep from his eyes, and eventually saunters out of the tent, much of the morning spent. With great effort he drags out a recliner to the top of the hill and lies back in it, much to the amazement of the chieftain and his people. He enjoys the view of the rich, fertile countryside as he eats a late brunch. He dozes off after the meal, then awakens some time later. With the sun now past the midpoint in the sky, he finally stands up, yawns, stretches, picks up the spade, and makes his way down the hill at a leisurely pace. Having traveled just a small distance, he digs his first hole. Then, exhausted from his brief exertion, he sits down to eat lunch. After lunch, he moves left a short distance and digs his second hole. Then, satisfied with his work, he disdains any further walking or digging and labors straight back up to the recliner and spends the rest of the day dozing.

If Jonathan Edwards were there, he would undoubtedly be screaming exhortations at such a Christian, pleading with him to expand his heavenly ambitions. He would beg all of us to "exert ourselves with all the power, might, vigor, and vehemence, yea violence, we are capable of" in acquiring heavenly real estate. He would want us to get up every day and do everything we do for the glory of God (1 Cor. 10:31). He would want us to exert ourselves toward personal holiness, putting sin to death by the Spirit (Rom. 8:13), thus expanding the dimensions of our heavenly pleasure. He would want us to be out trading with the talents of the gospel, seeking to multiply disciples with great zeal for their eternal good and God's eternal glory.

So I would rephrase Tolstoy's story title to this: "How Much Heaven Do You Want?" How much of God's glory do you want to experience in heaven? How large a measure of joy do you want in heaven? "With the measure you use it will be measured back to you" (Luke 6:38). Our self-denial now in favor of pursuing personal holiness and in service to the spread of the gospel will expand our capacity in heaven for delighting in and displaying the glory of God. And every good work we collect through diligent and sacrificial labor will receive our Father's specific and eternal approval in heaven. Forever he will say, "Well done, you good and faithful servant." How much of that do you want? As William Carey said of missions, "Expect great things from God; attempt great things for God!"[4] What about you? Are you running a race with great energy, making a circuit like Pahom but for far better and eternally lasting real estate? Or are you like the guy in the recliner squandering hours . . . and days . . . and years?

Benefits from Meditating on Heaven's Eternal History Lessons

Now that we have reached the end of our study together, how could a deep and scripturally saturated meditation on this concept of a dynamic heavenly review of earth's events affect the way we run our race and claim in God's name our portion of heavenly glory? Here are a few ways.

1. Total focus of all of our lives on the spread of the gospel. We should picture the time when we will see that multitude greater than anyone could count from all people groups across all eras of human history standing in white robes worshiping their Savior (Rev. 7:9). We should marshal our resources—our time, energy, money, spiritual gifts, opportunities—to do whatever we can to bring this about. Meditation on this heavenly theme will tend toward that end.

2. *Excitement that heaven is dynamic.* The more we think about this, the more exciting heaven will seem to us. Satan's depressing caricature of strumming harps eternally on a puffy white cloud will be driven forever from our minds. We will realize that heaven is far from boring, and that we will be eternally developing in our detailed and comprehensive knowledge of the glory of God.

3. *Redemption of our unique times.* We are commanded to "[redeem] the time, because the days are evil" (Eph. 5:16 KJV). The more aware we are of the detailed and comprehensive review of history that awaits us, the more precious and unique every single moment will seem.

4. *Increasing awareness of God's sovereign rule.* The more we meditate on these themes, the more aware we will be of God's sovereignty over human history—both the tiniest details (sparrows falling to the ground) and the most massive epochs (the rise and fall of world empires). This in turn will help us be stable in an eternal perspective and therefore more useful to God.

5. *Boldness in witness.* If the person we're witnessing to repents, we will have added one more brother or sister to the body of Christ for all eternity. If they persecute us, we will have added to our heavenly treasure trove. This perspective makes us increasingly fearless in the face of persecution, for Jesus wants us to "rejoice and be glad" when persecuted, knowing that "[our] reward is great in heaven" (Matt. 5:12).

6. *Less deceived about secret sin.* Like black mold, sin thrives in darkness. Satan deceives us that we are hidden when we are tempted. The more we think about the forthcoming heavenly review, the more aware we will be that "even the darkness is not dark" to God (Ps. 139:12) and that "there is nothing concealed that will not be revealed, or hidden that will not be known" (Matt. 10:26 NASB). So, *if you don't want to spend eternity remembering having done something, then don't do it!*

7. *Freedom from seeking earthly praise or rewards.* The more we realize that no good work we do on earth will ever be forgotten in heaven, the freer we will be from groveling for notice and praise now. We understand that God will celebrate even the hidden moments and obscure actions, and his praise is all we really want anyway (Rom. 2:29).

8. *Freedom from crippling sorrow over earthly loss.* The more mindful we are of the heavenly perspective on history, the freer we will be from grieving like those who have no hope (1 Thess. 4:13). We become increasingly confident that God has a reason for everything he does, and that in heaven we will finally understand. Therefore, we can be free from bitterness against God and free from asking "Why, O Lord?!"

9. *Freedom from burdensome sentimentality.* Some people are more sentimental than others. Some parents weep at weddings in part because the tender years of childhood are clearly and forever ended. Some cling to souvenirs and photos of moments that will never happen again. As their children grow up and stop using previously precious toys, parents tearfully store them in the attic for their grandkids. Many people say that if there were a house fire and everyone was safely out, the one thing they would save would be family

photos. But knowing that we will relive with heavenly perspective all the memories of life frees us up from clinging to the past. We can travel light as we move through this world. When my mother died recently, I found myself in the basement of her Cape Cod home with a little less than two hours to go through her vast repository of family photos. My siblings had already finished their selections, so it was down to me. This would be my last chance to grab these physical artifacts of my family's history. After I was done with my selection, the remainder would go to the dump. Yet I was not paralyzed by regret or frenzied by panic. The best and clearest reviews of my life await me in eternity. I made some selections, closed the boxes, and moved on.

10. *Deliverance from envy and boasting over fruitfulness.* It's easy for pastors like me to compare ministry success with other pastors . . . the size of their congregations, the number of baptisms, the variety of creative ministries. But in heaven we will be perfectly loving, and love "does not envy or boast" (1 Cor. 13:4). Instead, we will be one in Christ and will take pure delight in other people's honors as though they were our own.

11. *Understanding of unequal earthly circumstances.* Embracing the concept of variable levels of glory and honor in heaven helps us make sense of inequities in earthly conditions and see the hand of God in them. Some Christians suffer extremely in this world, through poverty, persecution, disasters, and other painful providences. They are being prepared for places of high honor (Matt. 20:23) and radiant glory through their manifestly greater sufferings. I can honor them even here and now—while seeking to emulate their courage and alleviate their earthly suffering.

12. Freedom from seeking revenge. Knowing that we will be vindicated eternally in reference to any human enemies we had on earth—either by their having been converted through our patient witness (as Saul of Tarsus was eventually, in part because of Stephen's powerful example [Acts 7:60]) or by their being justly condemned—frees us from any attempt at revenge.

13. Freedom from concern over Alzheimer's disease (or any memory loss). Alzheimer's disease is one of the most dreaded maladies in this world, for it seems to rob a person of their identity as a human being. They do not recognize even the most cherished loved ones—such as a spouse who has been tending them for years. But knowing that we will spend eternity in heaven with perfect memories frees us from any debilitating fear of this disease.

14. Freedom from concern that our lives will be forgotten in years to come. When the Lord takes us out of this world, it won't be long before our place remembers us no more (Ps. 103:16). But God will never forget even the smallest act done for his glorious kingdom, and all those acts will live in heavenly review for all eternity.

15. Ability to see intractable problems like poverty and racism in light of eternity. These evils stubbornly resist all efforts at transformation. The hearts of unconverted sinners are evil and beyond cure (Jer. 17:9), and the grief caused by both poverty and racism in every generation is incalculable. Heaven will be perfectly free from poverty and racism. More than that, we will remember these sins that caused so much grief in every generation, how all human efforts to solve them utterly failed, and that God solved them for his own glory only by the perfection of salvation in Christ. This heavenly hope does not make us fatalists who do nothing but rather energetic servants of that future kingdom who seek to alleviate these evils as much as possible, knowing they will finally be solved in heaven.

16. *Deeper desire to learn history now.* Studying Christian biographies is one of the most efficient uses of our time. They are inspirational, educational, and transformational. Given that we are going to spend eternity with these Christian heroes, it would behoove us in this world to learn as much as we can about them, so that we can "consider the outcome of their way of life, and imitate their faith" (Heb. 13:7).

17. *Freedom from needing to know the results of our faithfulness.* Paul said, "I planted the seed, Apollos watered it, but God has been making it grow" (1 Cor. 3:6 NIV). God often hides from us the full effects of our lives of service to him. The more we realize that heaven will reveal the full effects of the spiritual seeds we planted, the freer we will be from needing to know now. It is good for us to realize that we can't handle that full revelation now, because we are so arrogant. But God will show it to us in eternity.

18. *Reminder to cherish ordinary Christians and their good works.* If God will elevate some of the most obscure servants and their most hidden works and say that they, like the poor widow, "put in more than all the others" (Luke 21:3 NIV), then we should learn not to despise anyone's service to the Lord. We will realize that, as C. S. Lewis said,

There are no ordinary people. You have never talked to a mere mortal. Nations, cultures, arts, civilization—these are mortal, and their life is to ours as the life of a gnat. But it is immortals whom we joke with, work with, marry, snub, and exploit—immortal horrors or everlasting splendours.[5]

There are similarly no ordinary good works. The more we realize this dynamic, the humbler we will be toward other servants of Christ, and the more likely we will be to notice their works and thank and encourage them for each one.

19. Honor to women. History books are filled with the decisions and actions of men, while the lives and works of women—wives, mothers, singles—are often overlooked. If God cherishes the obscure works of ordinary people and assesses them to have put in more than all the others, this will especially be true of women. Heaven will be filled with the honors of women who labored and toiled in obscurity but whose self-sacrificial works effectively shaped and molded history.

20. Renewal of our strength. This meditation on heaven has consistently lifted my weary soul above my immediate circumstances, above any turbulent clouds of doubt and sorrow and seemingly insurmountable obstacles. This foretaste of heavenly glory is part of the down payment of my full inheritance delivered to me in a stipend check by the Holy Spirit (Eph. 1:14). And it has proven to have great power to renew my zeal for service to Christ.

Finally Answering the Vanity of Ecclesiastes

As we draw this study to a close, I want to highlight one of the greatest insights I've had concerning the power of meditating on heaven and the resurrection from the dead. It has to do with the word *vanity*, which appears again and again in the book of Ecclesiastes. Indeed, the theme of that book is asserted from the very beginning, then unfolded in great detail throughout the book: "Vanity of vanities, says the

Preacher, vanity of vanities! All is vanity" (Eccles. 1:2). He says it again later in that first chapter: "I have seen everything that is done under the sun, and behold, all is vanity and a striving after wind" (v. 14). This word translated "vanity" is also translated as "meaningless" (NIV) and "futile" (CSB).

The great fear of all energetic workers in this world is the sense that everything we do on earth is ultimately worthless. The phrase "a striving after wind" captures it well—constantly pursuing something that cannot be grasped, that really is effectively empty. To waste your life building something that ultimately will crumble and fall back into the dust from which we all came.

The great man who wrote Ecclesiastes, the wise King Solomon, walked through the many efforts he made to find meaning and purpose in his labors "under the sun." Especially galling to him was the concept that all his great projects—the houses and gardens and vineyards and parks that beautified his capital city—would have to be left behind when he died, and who knew whether his successor would be a wise man or a fool (2:18–19)? Death stood over all his works and mocked them all as dust in the wind. And once he was dead, it wouldn't be long before no one remembered what he had done at all . . . all physical trace of it would be gone, and no one alive would even remember that he had ever lived:

> A living dog is better than a dead lion. For the living know that they will die, but the dead know nothing, and they have no more reward, for the memory of them is forgotten. Their love and their hate and their envy have already perished, and forever they have no more share in all that is done under the sun. (9:4–6)

Just as perplexing to him was the fact that, no matter how wise he was or how much he studied what was done on earth, he could make no final sense of all of it. It seemed to be completely random and purposeless:

> I have seen the business that God has given to the children of man to be busy with. He has made everything beautiful in its time. Also, he has put eternity into man's heart, yet so that he cannot find out what God has done from the beginning to the end. (3:10–11)

But it was precisely here that God made a connection in my heart to Christ, the resurrection, and our heavenly education. Ecclesiastes uses a repeated phrase, "under the sun," meaning simply on Planet Earth. But I have seen that a better way to understand it is from the concept Paul refutes in 1 Corinthians 15, that there is no resurrection from the dead. If indeed there is no resurrection from the dead, if all that exists is life "under the sun," then life really is meaningless. But if Christ has been raised from the dead, then nothing we do for his kingdom is *in vain*. And Christ has indeed been raised from the dead! Therefore death cannot stand over our life's works and mock them. Rather we, the glorified saints, will see death itself thrown into the lake of fire (Rev. 20:14), and we will sing the victory taunt, "O death, where is your victory? O death, where is your sting?" (1 Cor. 15:55). Paul applies this radiant truth to our lives as Christians, and he answers the depressing "realism" of Ecclesiastes: "Therefore, my beloved brothers, be steadfast, immovable, always abounding in the work of the Lord, knowing that in the Lord your labor is not in vain" (v. 58).

That is the greatest daily application of this heavenly meditation. It means we can all be filled with a buoyant hope in our service to Christ day after day. Everything we do for the glory of God, whether great or small, famous or obscure, will be remembered in heaven and will shine for all eternity.

Notes

Chapter 1 Lost Treasures Reclaimed

1. C. Suetonius Tranquillus, "chapter 29," *Divus Augustus*, ed. Alexander Thomson, accessed April 7, 2021, http://www.perseus.tufts.edu/hopper/text?doc=Perseus%3Atext%3A1999.02.0132%3Alife%3Daug.%3Achapter%3D29.

2. Carrie Gracie, "Kublai Khan: China's Favourite Barbarian," *BBC News Magazine*, October 9, 2012, https://www.bbc.com/news/magazine-19850234.

3. I heard this statement from Erwin Lutzer, pastor of Moody Church, Chicago, in a private conversation at a Gospel Coalition stakeholders' meeting on the campus of Trinity Divinity School in 2006. Since then, I have heard others say Adrian Rogers said it in a sermon.

4. Randy Alcorn, *Heaven* (Carol Stream, IL: Tyndale, 2004), 5–6.

5. Valerie Tarico, "Ten Reasons Christian Heaven Would Actually Be Hell," Salon, February 1, 2015, https://www.salon.com/2015/02/01/10_reasons_christian_heaven_could_actually_be_hell_partner/.

Chapter 2 Biblical Proof of Heavenly Memories

1. John Calvin, *Institutes of the Christian Religion*, vol. 2, ed. John T. McNeill (Philadelphia: Westminster Press, 1960), 1005.

2. India Today Web Desk, "Srinivasa Ramanujan: The Mathematical Genius Who Credited His 3900 Formulae to Visions from Goddess Mahalakshmi," *India Today*, April 26, 2017, https://www.indiatoday.in

/education-today/gk-current-affairs/story/srinivasa-ramanujan-life-story
-973662-2017-04-26.

Chapter 3 Resurrected Bodies, Minds, and Hearts

1. Jonathan Edwards, "On the Unreasonableness of Indetermination in Religion," in *Sermons and Discourses 1734–1738*, ed. M. X. Lesser (New Haven: Yale University Press, 2001), 93.

2. Jonathan Edwards, "Personal Narrative," *A Jonathan Edwards Reader*, ed. John E. Smith, Harry S. Stout, and Kenneth P. Minkema (New Haven: Yale University Press, 1995), 293.

3. Iain H. Murray, *Jonathan Edwards: A New Biography* (Edinburgh: Banner of Truth Trust, 1987), 195.

4. John C. Pollock, *Moody: A Biographical Portrait* (New York: Macmillan, 1963), 90. It is interesting to note that Moody began to seek a greater sense of the presence and power of God in direct response to two obscure women who prayed for him to receive the power of the Holy Spirit: Sarah Anne Cooke and a widow named Mrs. Hawxhurst. They sat in the front row of a tent meeting Moody was preaching at, and remained a long time afterward praying for him. When Moody went to talk with them, and they told him they were praying for him to receive the power of the Holy Spirit, Moody became slightly offended and said, "Why don't you pray for the people?" They answered, "Because you need the power of the Spirit." This had a big effect on Moody, and he began to pray as never before for the moving of the Spirit in his life. It reached a climax when he said he really did not want to live anymore without it. In November 1871, he was walking down a very busy street in New York City (maybe Broadway or Fifth Avenue) and a sense of the presence of God started to flood his mind. He hurried to be alone to pray. He went to a friend's house, brushed aside his invitation to a meal, and went to a solitary room. Pollock writes, "Moody locked the door and sat on the sofa. The room seemed ablaze with God. Moody dropped to the floor and lay bathing in the divine."

5. Augustine, *Confessions*, book 1, chapter 6, trans. R. S. Pine-Coffin (Middlesex, UK: Penguin, 1986), 25.

6. John Piper, "Getting to the Bottom of Your Joy: Message from Passion 2011, Atlanta," Desiring God, January 3, 2011, https://www.desiring god.org/messages/getting-to-the-bottom-of-your-joy.

7. John Piper, "Charles Spurgeon: Preaching Through Adversity, 1995 Bethlehem Conference for Pastors," Desiring God, January 31, 1995, https://www.desiringgod.org/messages/charles-spurgeon-preaching -through-adversity.

Chapter 4 Better Than Virtual Reality

1. Jake Swearingen, "Virtual Reality Lets You Escape the World. Augmented Reality Improves It," *Post Reality*, January 21, 2019, http://nymag.com/intelligencer/2019/01/augmented-reality-vs-virtual-reality-the-future-of-tech.html.

2. Jeff Hurt, "Your Senses Are Your Raw Information Learning Portals," Velvet Chainsaw Consulting, May 23, 2012, https://velvetchainsaw.com/2012/05/23/your-senses-your-raw-information-learning-portals. See also Lawrence D. Rosenblum, *See What I'm Saying: The Extraordinary Powers of Our Five Senses* (New York: W. W. Norton, 2011).

3. Charles Dickens, *A Christmas Carol: A Ghost Story of Christmas* (Auckland, NZ: Floating Press, 2009), 48–49.

Chapter 5 Rewards

1. *Patton*, directed by Franklin J. Schaffner (Twentieth Century Fox, 1970).

2. Keith Green, "Oh Lord, You're Beautiful," *So You Wanna Go Back to Egypt* (Pretty Good Music, 1980).

3. Jonathan Edwards, "Heaven Is a World of Love," in *Charity and Its Fruits* (Carlisle, PA: Banner of Truth Trust, 2005), 336.

4. Edwards, "Heaven Is a World of Love," 336, 338.

5. Edwards, "Heaven Is a World of Love," 336.

6. Edwards, "Heaven Is a World of Love."

7. Edwards, "Heaven Is a World of Love," 337.

Chapter 6 God's Sovereign Weaving of the Tapestry of History

1. Andrew Davis, *The Power of Christian Contentment* (Grand Rapids: Baker Books, 2019), 138.

2. Gerald Beals, "Thomas Edison 'Quotes,'" ThomasEdison.com, accessed December 6, 2020, https://www.thomasedison.com/quotes.html.

3. Daniel Merritt, "Voltaire's Prediction, Home, and the Bible Society: Truth or Myth? Further Evidence of Verification," Cross Examined, accessed December 11, 2020, https://crossexamined.org/voltaires-prediction-home-and-the-bible-society-truth-or-myth-further-evidence-of-verification/.

Chapter 7 Honoring Heroes, Worshiping God

1. I wrote these words down while standing in front of the statue. I later found out they were a variant of Prospero's lines from Shakespeare's *The Tempest* (Act IV, Scene 1).

2. Jonathan Edwards, "Treatise Concerning Religious Affections," in *The Works of Jonathan Edwards*, vol. 1, ed. Patrick H. Alexander (Peabody, MA: Hendrickson, 2000), 237.

3. The full quote is from Athanasius, *On the Incarnation of the Word*: "And in a word, the achievements of the Savior, resulting from his becoming man, are of such kind and number that if one should wish to enumerate them, he may be compared to men who gaze at the expanse of the sea and wish to count its waves. For as one cannot take in the whole of the waves with his eyes, for those which are coming on baffle the sense of him that attempts it; so for him that would take in all the achievements of Christ in the body, it is impossible to take in the whole, even by reckoning them up, as those which go beyond his thought are more than those he thinks he has taken in. Better is it, then, not to aim at speaking of the whole, where one cannot do justice even to a part, but, after mentioning one more, to leave the whole for you to marvel at. For all alike are marvelous, and wherever a man turns his glance, he may behold on that side the divinity of the Word, and be struck with exceeding great awe." As quoted by John Piper, *21 Servants of Sovereign Joy* (Wheaton, IL: Crossway, 2018), 394.

4. The most readable and comprehensive book I would recommend is Bruce L. Shelley, *Church History in Plain Language*, 4th ed. (Nashville: Nelson, 2013).

5. Justo L. Gonzalez, *The Story of Christianity*, vol. 1 (New York: HarperCollins, 1984), 44.

6. Gonzalez, *Story of Christianity*, 46.

7. Piper, *21 Servants*, 397–98.

8. Shelley, *Church History in Plain Language*, 279.

9. Steven Lawson, "William Tyndale's Final Words," Ligonier Ministries, February 18, 2015, https://www.ligonier.org/blog/william-tyndales-final-words/.

10. "Lucid brevity" was Calvin's goal as stated in his "Dedication to Simon Grynaeus," in *Commentary on Romans*, trans. Ross Mackenzie (Grand Rapids: Eerdmans, 1980), 1.

11. John Knox, "Letter to Anne Locke, 1556," in *The Works of John Knox*, vol. 4, ed. David Laing (Eugene, OR: Wipf & Stock, 2004), 240.

12. John Owen, "The Death of Death in the Death of Christ," in *The Works of John Owen*, vol. 10, ed. William H. Goold (Carlisle, PA: Banner of Truth Trust, 1993).

13. John Bunyan, "Grace Abounding to the Chief of Sinners," in *The Works of John Bunyan*, vol. 1, ed. George Offor (Carlisle, PA: Banner of Truth Trust, 1991), 10.

14. Randy and Cathy Colver, "The Quotable Whitefield," *Christianity Today*, accessed December 8, 2020, https://www.christianitytoday.com /history/issues/issue-38/quotable-whitefield.html.

15. Joseph Belcher, *George Whitefield: A Biography* (New York: American Tract Society, 1857), 317; https://www.gutenberg.org/files/44140/44140 -h/44140-h.htm.

16. David Brainerd, "The Life and Diary of the Rev. David Brainerd," in *The Works of Johnathan Edwards*, vol. 2, ed. Patrick H. Alexander (Peabody, MA: Hendrickson, 2000), 313–458.

17. Courtney Anderson, *To the Golden Shore* (Boston: Little, Brown and Co., 1956).

18. "George Müller: Trusting God for Daily Bread," Harvest Ministry, accessed December 8, 2020, http://harvestministry.org/muller.

19. Dr. and Mrs. Howard Taylor, *Hudson Taylor's Spiritual Secret* (London: China Inland Mission, 1935), 11–12.

20. Charles Spurgeon, *C. H. Spurgeon Autobiography: The Early Years*, vol. 1 (Carlisle, PA: Banner of Truth Trust, 1981), 534. Many thanks to Philip McDuffie for helping me locate this story! (And the next one!)

21. Charles Spurgeon, *Spurgeon's Sermons*, vols. 7–8 (Grand Rapids: Baker Books, 2007), 234.

22. "Dwight L. Moody: Revivalist with a Common Touch," *Christianity Today*, accessed December 9, 2020, https://www.christianitytoday.com /history/people/evangelistsandapologists/dwight-l-moody.html.

23. Faris Daniel Whitesell, "D. L. Moody, the Practical Personal Worker," Wholesome Words, accessed December 9, 2020, https://www.wholesome words.org/biography/biomoody12.html.

24. Brother Andrew, with John and Elizabeth Sherrill, *God's Smuggler* (Bloomington, MN: Chosen Books, 2015), 82–91.

25. Elisabeth Elliot, *Shadow of the Almighty: The Life and Testament of Jim Elliot* (Grand Rapids: Zondervan, 1970), 108.

Chapter 8 Obscure People and Events Finally Revealed

1. Eric Bogle, "No Man's Land," ©1980 by Larrikin Music.

2. Missions historian Edward L. Smither writes, "We know almost nothing about the origins of the African church. We have no record of early missionaries or church planters—only the emergence of a vibrant church in the late second and early third century. . . . In 220, Bishop Agrippinus of Carthage presided over a church council attended by seventy bishops from a single African province (Proconsular Africa). Since there were seventy churches in one African province and many more in the rest of Roman Africa, this signified much growth in the early third-century

church. Even more remarkable, this council occurred just forty years after the first literary reference to Christianity in Africa—the account of the martyrs of Scilli condemned at Carthage in 180. Interestingly, a majority of these twelve martyrs (seven men and five women) bore indigenous African (Punic-Berber) names, indicating that the church had penetrated the African interior, evidence that Christianity was surely present in North Africa well before 180. . . . So the origins of the African church are quite early (early second century), and the missionaries who brought the gospel are strikingly anonymous. These early evangelists were most likely made up of merchants, colonists, and even soldiers whose work brought them to Africa." Edward L. Smither, *Christian Mission: A Concise Global History* (Bellingham, WA: Lexham Press, 2019), 24–25.

3. David J. Brady, *Not Forgotten: Inspiring Missionary Pioneers* (Maitland, FL: Xulon Press, 2018), 1–18.

4. Brady, *Not Forgotten*, 114–24.

5. The key primary source text for the life of James Gilmour is Richard Lovett, *James Gilmour of Mongolia: His Diaries, Letters, and Reports* (London: The Religious Tract Society, 1892). See also John C. Lambert, *The Adventure of Missionary Heroism* (San Antonio, TX: Vision Forum Inc., 2005), 3–19.

6. Lovett, *James Gilmour of Mongolia*, 206.

7. Lovett, *James Gilmour of Mongolia*, 161–62.

8. Lovett, *James Gilmour of Mongolia*, 163.

9. Lovett, *James Gilmour of Mongolia*, 224.

10. Thor Heyerdahl, *Kon-Tiki: Across the Pacific in a Raft* (New York: Rand McNally, 1951).

11. Andrew Davis, "Are People without Christ Really Lost?" in *God's Love Compels Us: Taking the Gospel to the World*, ed. D. A. Carson and Kathleen Nielson (Wheaton, IL: Crossway, 2015), 99.

12. *A Hidden Life*, directed by Terrence Malick (Fox Searchlight Pictures, 2019).

13. George Eliot, *Middlemarch* (repr. London: Oxford University Press, 2019), 785.

Chapter 9 Spiritual Dimensions Unveiled

1. Paul Hiebert, "The Flaw of the Excluded Middle," *Missiology: An International Review* 10 (1982): 35–47.

2. Roland H. Bainton, *Here I Stand: A Life of Martin Luther* (Nashville: Abingdon Press, 1950), 19.

3. Bainton, *Here I Stand*, 150.

4. Bainton, *Here I Stand*, 181.

5. Martin Brecht, *Martin Luther: His Road to Reformation 1483–1521*, trans. James L. Schaaf (Minneapolis: Fortress Press, 1993), 453–56.

6. Bainton, *Here I Stand*, 144.

7. A. W. Tozer, *The Knowledge of the Holy* (San Francisco: Harper-Collins, 1978), 70.

8. Andrew M. Davis, *Exalting Jesus in Isaiah: Christ-Centered Exposition* (Nashville: B&H, 2017), 95–97.

9. William L. Shirer, *The Rise and Fall of the Third Reich* (New York: Simon & Schuster, 2011), 391.

10. See Revelation 13; 1 John 2:18–22; 4:3; 2 John 7; 2 Thessalonians 2:8; Daniel 7:8.

11. See Bertin M. Louis Jr., "Haiti's Pact with the Devil? (Some Haitians Believe This Too)," The Immanent Frame, February 18, 2010, https://tif.ssrc.org/2010/02/18/haitis-pact-with-the-devil-some-haitians-believe-this-too.

12. C. S. Lewis, *The Screwtape Letters* (New York: Macmillan, 1961), 64–65.

13. John Bunyan, *The Pilgrim's Progress*, ed. W. R. Owens (Oxford: Oxford University Press, 2003), 65.

14. Bunyan, *Pilgrim's Progress*, 32.

Chapter 10 Of Personal Interest

1. This is true of the Hinayana branch of Buddhism, which conceives of nirvana as "extinction" or "blowing out": "the annihilation of sorrow, desire, and finally the illusion of self." It is a pure nothingness described as a "dreamless sleep in which the sleeping man does not know himself, nor that he exists, nor that he knows anything at all," in A. L. Herman, *An Introduction to Buddhist Thought* (Lanham, MD: University Press of America, 1983), 248–49. Other sects of Buddhism reject such a view.

2. John Murray, *Redemption Accomplished and Applied* (Grand Rapids: Eerdmans, 1955).

3. Davis, *Power of Christian Contentment*, 55.

4. John Flavel, "The Mystery of Providence," in *The Works of John Flavel*, vol. 4 (Carlisle, PA: Banner of Truth Trust, 1997), 340.

5. Michael Boland, "Introduction," in John Flavel, *The Mystery of Divine Providence* (Edinburgh: Banner of Truth Trust, 1963), 11.

Chapter 11 Our Sins Redeemed and Painlessly Remembered

1. Thomas Watson, *The Doctrine of Repentance* (Carlisle, PA: Banner of Truth Trust, 1994), 39.

2. Watson, *Doctrine of Repentance*, 44.

Chapter 12 Our Earthly Sufferings Fully Explained

1. Anderson, *Golden Shore*, 359.

2. Anderson, *Golden Shore*, 378.

3. As quoted in Michael E. Rusten and Sharon Rusten, *The One Year Christian History* (Carol Stream, IL: Tyndale, 2003); http://reformedangli cans.blogspot.com/2015/09/20-september-1542-ad-dr-martin-luther .html.

4. As quoted in "The American Colony in Jerusalem: Family Tragedy," Library of Congress Exhibits, accessed December 9, 2020, https://www .loc.gov/exhibits/americancolony/amcolony-family.html.

5. Jonathan Edwards, *The Works of Jonathan Edwards: Letters and Personal Writings*, vol. 16, ed. George S. Claghorn (New Haven: Yale University Press, 1998), 66.

6. Arnold Dallimore, *Spurgeon: A New Biography* (Carlisle, PA: Banner of Truth Trust, 1995), 69–72.

7. Matt Corley, "Hagee Says Hurricane Katrina Struck New Orleans Because It Was 'Planning a Sinful Homosexual Rally,'" Think Progress, accessed December 9, 2020, https://archive.thinkprogress .org/hagee-says-hurricane-katrina-struck-new-orleans-because-it-was -planning-a-sinful-homosexual-rally-55b392a04322/. See also Catherine Wessinger, "Religious Responses to the Katrina Disaster in New Orleans and the American Gulf Coast," *Journal of Religious Studies, Japanese Association for Religious Studies* 86–2, no. 373 (September 2012): 53–83.

8. Bunyan, "Grace Abounding," 7.

9. Richard Cecil, "Memoirs of the Rev. John Newton," in *The Works of the Rev. John Newton*, vol. 1 (Edinburgh: Banner of Truth, 1985), 25.

10. "A War Story: 'There Is No Pit So Deep God's Love Is Not Deeper Still,'" Christian History Institute, accessed March 19, 2021, https://chris tianhistoryinstitute.org/magazine/article/there-is-no-pit-so-deep.

11. "Severe Acute Respiratory Syndrome (SARS)," Centers for Disease Control and Prevention, accessed December 9, 2020, https://www.cdc .gov/sars/about/fs-sars.html.

12. The Visual and Data Journalism Team, "Covid Map: Coronavirus Cases, Deaths, Vaccinations by Country," *BBC News*, accessed December 9, 2020, https://www.bbc.com/news/world-51235105.

13. Jared Diamond, *Guns, Germs, and Steel: The Fates of Human Societies* (New York: W. W. Norton, 1999), 77.

14. Nik Ripken, *The Insanity of God* (Nashville: B&H, 2013).

15. Nik Ripken, "My Son Died Today," Nik Ripken Ministries, March 26, 2013, https://www.nikripken.com/the-death-of-a-son/.

16. Ripken, *Insanity of God*, 42.

17. J. I. Packer, *Knowing God* (Downers Grove, IL: InterVarsity Press, 1973), 92.

18. Packer, *Knowing God*, 97.

19. "God Moves in a Mysterious Way," William Cowper (1774), public domain.

Chapter 13 Memories of the Damned

1. Iain Murray, *Spurgeon: The Early Years* (Edinburgh: Banner of Truth, 1962), 44.

2. Alexandre Dumas, *The Count of Monte Cristo*, trans. David Coward (Oxford: Oxford University Press, 2008), 341–42.

3. Anderson, *Golden Shore*, 248–51.

Chapter 14 The Consummation of Our Education in Evil

1. David A. Koplow, *Smallpox: The Fight to Eradicate a Global Scourge* (Berkeley: University of California Press, 2003); Pat Bailey, "Epidemics on the Horizon," *UC Davis Magazine* (Summer 2006), http://magazinearchive.ucdavis.edu/issues/su06/feature_1.html; "How Poxviruses Such as Smallpox Evade the Immune System," Science-Daily, February 1, 2008, https://www.sciencedaily.com/releases/2008/01/080131122956.htm.

2. "What Is the Source of the Phrase 'Never Again'?" Mosaic, accessed April 15, 2021, https://mosaicmagazine.com/observation/history-ideas/2017/06/what-is-the-source-of-the-phrase-never-again/.

3. Emily Burack, "'Never Again': From a Holocaust Phrase to a Universal Phrase," *Jerusalem Post*, March 10, 2018, https://www.jpost.com/diaspora/never-again-from-a-holocaust-phrase-to-a-universal-phrase-544666.

4. George Santayana, "Reason in Common Sense," in *The Life of Reason; or The Phases of Human Progress* (London: Constable & Co., 1906), 284.

5. "The Book of the Thousand Nights and One Night / The Man Who Never Laughed Again," Wikisource, accessed December 9, 2020, https://en.wikisource.org/wiki/The_Book_of_the_Thousand_Nights_and_One_Night/The_Man_Who_Never_Laughed_Again.

Chapter 15 Applications

1. Edwards, *Works of Jonathan Edwards*, vol. 16, 754.

2. Edwards, "Heaven Is a World of Love," 336.

3. Leo Tolstoy, *How Much Land Does a Man Need? And Other Stories*, trans. Ronald Wilks (London: Penguin Books, 1993).

4. "Friar Lane Baptist Chapel: Site of William Carey's Deathless Sermon," Carey Center, accessed April 15, 2021, https://www.wmcarey.edu/carey/friarlane/friar.htm.

5. C. S. Lewis, *The Weight of Glory, and Other Addresses* (New York: Macmillan, 1949), 15.

Dr. Andrew M. Davis, a native of Boston, MA, is the senior pastor of First Baptist Church of Durham, NC, and the founder of Two Journeys Ministry. He holds a bachelor's degree from MIT, a Masters of Divinity from Gordon-Conwell Theological Seminary, and a PhD from Southern Baptist Theological Seminary. He is also a visiting professor of church history at Southeastern Baptist Theological Seminary, a counsel member of The Gospel Coalition, and a trustee of the International Mission Board. In addition to his preaching and teaching, he is the author of *An Approach to the Extended Memorization of Scripture, An Infinite Journey: Growing Toward Christlikeness, Revitalize: Biblical Keys to Helping Your Church Come Alive Again, Christ Centered Exposition: Exalting Jesus in Isaiah*, and *The Power of Christian Contentment: Finding Deeper, Richer Christ-Centered Joy*. He and his wife, Christi, reside in Bahama, NC, and have five children and two grandchildren.

You can find his work at

FBCDurham.org

TwoJourneys.org

Also Available from
ANDREW M. DAVIS

"I can't recall ever making this statement about a book:
CHURCH LEADERS NEED THIS."
—THOM S. RAINER, president and CEO, LifeWay Christian Resources

BakerBooks
a division of Baker Publishing Group
www.BakerBooks.com

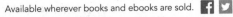 Available wherever books and ebooks are sold.

THE CURE TO
CHRONIC RESTLESSNESS

"If there was ever a time a distracted and exhausted
church needed this message, it is today."

—J. D. GREEAR,
pastor, The Summit Church, Raleigh-Durham, NC;
former president, Southern Baptist Convention

a division of Baker Publishing Group
www.BakerBooks.com

Available wherever books and ebooks are sold.

Helping Christians Make Progress

Sermons — Classes — Podcasts — Bible Studies

www.twojourneys.org

Advocate for Gospel-Centered Principles and Practices

To learn more, visit
www.TheGospelCoalition.org

Connect with

BakerBooks

Relevant. Intelligent. Engaging.

Sign up for announcements about
new and upcoming titles at

BakerBooks.com/SignUp

@ReadBakerBooks